Unsupported Assertions

Also by Hugh Hood

NOVELS

White Figure, White Ground 1964
The Camera Always Lies 1967
A Game of Touch 1970
You Cant Get There from Here 1972
Five New Facts About Giorgione 1987

"THE NEW AGE/LE NOUVEAU SIECLE"

I: *The Swing in the Garden* 1975
II: *A New Athens* 1977
III: *Reservoir Ravine* 1979
IV: *Black and White Keys* 1982
V: *The Scenic Art* 1984
VI: *The Motor Boys in Ottawa* 1986
VII: *Tony's Book* 1988
VIII: *Property and Value* 1990

STORIES

Flying a Red Kite 1962
Around the Mountain: Scenes from Montreal Life 1967
The Fruit Man, the Meat Man and the Manager 1971
Dark Glasses 1976
Selected Stories 1978
None Genuine without This Signature 1980
August Nights 1985
A Short Walk in the Rain 1989
The Isolation Booth 1991

NON-FICTION

Strength Down Centre: The Jean Beliveau Story 1970
The Governor's Bridge Is Closed 1973
Scoring: Seymour Segal's Art of Hockey 1979
Trusting the Tale 1983
Unsupported Assertions 1991

Unsupported Assertions

Hugh Hood

Essays

"Genius is only a series of unsupported assertions..."
Anon.

For Marshall McLuhan

Copyright © 1991 by Hugh Hood

Published in 1991 by
House of Anansi Press Limited
1800 Steeles Avenue West
Concord, Ontario
L4K 2P3

Canadian Cataloguing in Publication Data

Hood, Hugh, 1928-
Unsupported assertions

ISBN 0-88784-162-7 (bound) ISBN 0-88784-505-3 (pbk.)

I.Title.

PS8515.063U5 1991 C814'.54 C91-093308-1
PR9199.3.H66U5 1991

Cover Design: Brant Cowie/Artplus

Printed in Canada

CONTENTS

Authority in Canada *1*

The Idea of a Canadian Tradition *10*

Our Lost Vienna *20*

The War against the Fetus *30*

Cher in Bologna: McLuhan Revisited *40*

Memory Games, or, How to Bring It All Back *50*

The Persistence of Romanticism *60*

History as Myth *70*

Practical Formalism: Mining the Sentence *81*

What Is the Difference between Thinking and Feeling? *92*

Televisic, Dramatic, Cinematic *102*

The Intuition of Being: Morley, Marshall and Me *112*

Authority in Canada

Never mind the two-party system; what Canadians really like is government by a ruling party that generously permits occasional interruptions by a completely co-opted, institutionalized opposition party with the revolutionary thrust of a sagging sexual member. A party composed of progressive conservatives — that is, of people who would like to have the best of all possible political worlds while fearlessly straddling the fence. The ruling party here and there calls itself conservative or sometimes liberal but what it ought to be called is simply The Ruling Party, an organization bowed down to and worshipped by all right-thinking Canadians — that is, all Canadians. British Columbia under the Bennetts, Alberta under Lougheed, Québec under Duplessis, Ontario under Frost, Robarts and Davis, the federal government under Macdonald, Laurier, King or Trudeau supply examples of single-party rule and "official" democracy that recall the Republicanism of the late nineteenth-century Midwest in the United States. Ontario is just Ohio with a few letters added. Even Mr. Rae's new NDP government seems about to melt into the Canadian orthodoxy of authority.

Imagine rich, powerful, populous, free Ontario subjecting itself to the rule of a monolithic single party for more than forty years. Beats Romania! How could Ontarians fall for it? How could they fail to understand that any government, no matter how innocuous, how benevolent, that is left in power for forty years will halfway through its life become hopelessly mired in all sorts of irresponsible administrative encrustations? The Milk Board, the Egg Marketing Board, the nuclear-energy lobby, the lunatic fringe of the Highways Department busy building expressways from nowhere to nowhere, special interests like the provincial universities? In Québec M. Duplessis was frank about his curtailment of personal freedom. In Eastern Ontario if you belong to a co-operative cheese factory you may not exceed its quota by supplying it with your surplus milk production, which has to be poured down the drain. The future of the independent cheese producer shrinks and shrinks, and one of the glories of the rural economy of Ontario, a superb Cheddar, disappears from the supermarkets as Kraft looms larger and larger.

That isn't progress; we are not a progressive people. What we adore is things as they are, or better, as they were about three months ago, not excessively far in the past and not, God help us, any distance in the future. We display a profound and richly suggestive need of strong, stable regimes that will tell us what we must think and how we must feel. We have made the public authority into an idol. What do Canadians desire of their governments and public institutions? What do they hope to hear from them? The trend-setting bank rate. The correct social line, the right way to think, the titles of the right books to read and the right films to see. A body of Canadian professors of Canadian literature once took it upon itself to list the hundred best Canadian novels, and Canadians were perfectly ready to accept and enshrine this list by fastening it to refrigerator doors with magnets, then start reading down the list in all seriousness. I know about this because a novel of mine was named about ninety-seventh on the list. Not too many Canadian readers persisted that far down the officially approved roster. There can be no place for an excessive persistence in our country, and there must be something un-Canadian about a ninety-seventh-best novel.

Sometimes a minority coalesces to rig a nominating convention so that their candidate gets to run for office. Once in office however, the minority representative melts into the crowd of back benchers at the edge of the TV screen and that's the last we see or hear of him or her. It is obligatory in 1990 to write "him or her" or better "her or him" because the superficial counsels of media-born programmatic feminism tell us that we must do so. We may not address a woman as Miss. Horrors! Imagine referring to Sheila Copps as Miss Copps. The sky would fall.

The slave mentality was first and best described by Friedrich Nietzsche, but nobody in Canada is reading Nietzsche, or if she does she's keeping it dark.

Instead we profess a dogmatic orthodoxy enforced by authoritative communications media like the two major chains of newspapers, the CBC radio and television networks and a system of minor persuaders and arm-twisters such as the proliferating arts boards and other granting bodies. We give agonized attention to the series of international wrongdoings paraded before us by interested publicists like the noisy David Suzuki, the woes of black South Africans; the destruction of vast ranges of our physical environment; militaristic insurgency in Central and South America. "Remove first the beam which is in thine own eye" ought to be pinned up on every Canadian refrigerator door beside the official roster of readable Canadian novels, more especially on the refrigerator door of the official residence of any Canadian minister for External Affairs, that faceless functionary whose unending task it is to meddle in other nations' business, telling them what they ought to do.

Fais ce que dois. Slogan or motto of the best Canadian newspaper. I'm not allowed to call *Le Devoir* a Canadian newspaper, and the Montréal *Gazette* informs me that it is wrong to speak of French Canadians, but what the hell, I'll risk it. *Le Devoir* is the best Canadian newspaper, remaining almost unbearably boring over any period longer than the inside of a week because of its unalterably self-righteous tone, best evoked by translating its slogan as "Do what you ought!" We have too many voices like that, telling us what we ought to do and ought to think.

We were led to believe that Liona Boyd, bless her, was a virtuoso guitarist, whereas in fact this engaging instrumentalist has never been able to execute correctly pieces in any tempo quicker than a dignified *allegro moderato*. It would be heresy to note that after twenty years of it Karen Kain no longer possesses the physical resources of a prima ballerina. The Canadian Brass is not a world-class instrumental ensemble; it's a group of posing clowns.

Le Devoir commands us to do as we ought — that is, in accordance with the clearly grasped commands of conscience. Okay, I can handle that. But it's all we ever hear from our rulers, except for the even stronger admonition "Do as you're told!" Have the proper opinions and tastes!

Arthur Meighen was a Shakespearean scholar.

There are no French Canadians.

Glenn Gould was a posturing neurotic.

Anne of Green Gables is a major work of art.

George Grant was a philosopher.

Marshall McLuhan was a crank with a gift for self-advertisement.

The Globe and Mail is our national newspaper.

The University of Toronto is the Harvard of Canada.

None of the last eight statements is true.

The French call people like us *les bien-pensants*, the right-thinking element who would sooner die than hold unofficial opinions, who know in their hearts that Liona Boyd has outgone Segovia, that Lucy Maud rivals Charles Dickens, that Vincent Massey possessed a country house along the lines of Longleat or Castle Howard and was himself an aristocrat. Challenged to give an example of a Canadian aristocrat, a student of mine suggested Vincent Massey! There is no upper class in Canada, thank God! The weight of duly instructed conscience upon our poor harassed lives is already too heavy for us to bear any longer without extensive social neurosis and grave repression; we are hagridden (taking hags to be of either sex) by hatred of ourselves. We don't hate our fellow citizens, Pakistanis, Quebecers, boat people. What we really hate and detest and despise is ourselves as reflected in them. We are from sea to sea a nation of self-haters. To regard *Anne of Green Gables* as a major work of Canadian children's literature, or Canadian literature of any sort, is the sheerest self-hatred. It is to deconstruct radically our intelligence and taste.

Bad art comes into existence to pander to social fear; that's why Pope and Swift hated it so vigorously. Bad art, like mass neurosis, shackles the free imagination and conscience, and has awful consequences for the people. Think of Hitlerian architecture or the Stalinist proscription of Shostakovich. If you are fed an unvarying diet of Lucy Maud, Toller Cranston TV specials, policy statements by Brian Mulroney, quartet performances by the bungling Orford String Quartet, discussions of the state of the arts by Otto Jelinek, critical dissertations by Bobby Fulford, your head will begin to throb under the punishment. In the end you'll be talking like Muhammad Ali. Your sense of the ridiculous will be atrophied and your intelligence, imagination and feelings will lapse into muddy crudity. You may get to like "Lance et compte" or the comedy of "Rock et belles oreilles" or "Codco" or hockey telecasts.

When was there a Canadian voter revolution? The NDP victory in Ontario, Mohawk unrest in Quebec, record low support for the present federal government suggest that one may be on the way, but until now the closest thing to it has been the rise of the Parti Egalité/Equality Party in Quebec to a position of considerable power and influence in the Assemblée Nationale. The élite of Westmount — if that be not a contradiction in terms — refused to vote for their Equality Party candidate in the recent provincial election, because his election would have compromised their status as an obedient sub-élite. Working-class voters and a few activists like Mordecai Richler shoehorned Richard Holden into the assembly in the company of a veteran broadcaster, a CEGEP history teacher and a professional architect of twenty-nine years. Two of them bilingual, two monolingual, all four are currently functioning on key committees in Québec and beginning to make their presence felt in the legislative chamber very distinctly.

During the election campaign *The Globe and Mail* came out fearlessly and strongly against the Equality Party, against the very idea that a group of ordinary citizens like you and me should take it upon themselves to try to reverse established voting patterns. *The Globe and Mail* knew nothing whatsoever about the convictions of the English-language voter in Québec. All the editorial staff knew was that the conventional distribution of votes was being called into question, boat-rocking that must at all costs be disallowed. I call that an offensive intrusion in the lives of free citizens by an organ that claims to speak with a commanding voice, without the smallest shadow of a right to do so. Who cares what the editorialists on *The Globe and Mail* think? Most Canadian

6

newspaper readers, that's who. Imagine forming your opinions on the counsels of Jeffrey Simpson!

We have made a popular sideshow out of our most influential police agency, at once to salve our consciences and to reassure ourselves, in accordance with our myth of pacific obedience, that no Canadian police could ever be capable of dirty tricks. Our Mounties ride handsome horses and wear handsome coats and couldn't possibly be up to anything questionable like trying to silence journalists by laying untenable charges. The policeman is your friend. Sure he is!

How can we persuade ourselves that the RCMP is all goodness and innocence, and high visibility on horseback? Pure Canadianism, that's what that is. The really powerful and dangerous forces in our lives must be seen to be innocent, colourful and good, like the Mounties and the banks, those caring folks with the towering head offices and the high profit margins.

Is there a corner of Canada free from authoritarian submissiveness? Not Ontario with its forty years of the big blue machine, its ready employment of political managers like Hugh David Segal and its complaisant socialists. British Columbia? B.C. went out and found its Reagan clone and now has discovered that the robot has come dreadfully to life, when all they wanted was another likeness of W. A. C. Bennett. Alberta, the oil gang? From Getty to Getty with never a pause to guess what's going on. Grant Devine? Gary Filmon? Somebody described the American intelligentsia as a herd of independent minds. The Canadian publicist belongs to a gaggle of Canada geese.

What causes this perpetually undignified posture? A few guesses might be made about its historical sources. Too-long-continued colonial status. Second-rank status among North American nations. (Foreign journalists always refer to the U.S.A. as "America" and

now Canadians are starting to do the same.) The un-
wholesome predominance of authoritarian Christianity
— Scots Presbyterianism and French Catholicism — in
our morals and manners. I speak as a believing and prac-
tising Catholic. The root of the matter requires careful
attention, but the fact of the behaviour, the outward and
visible cringing, remains undeniable.

One of the Montreal cable TV services recently found
that it could save large amounts of money by substitut-
ing the programming of the ETV station in Plattsburgh,
N.Y., for that of the corresponding station across Lake
Champlain in Burlington, Vermont. No market survey
was made, no inquiry about the tastes and preferences
of the stations' viewers. The switch in services was made
almost from one day to the next, without advance notice.
Cable subscribers simply found that a much-admired
and much-watched station had been taken off, and another, far less popular station put in its place. The cable
service, Vidéotron, in face of loud and resentful objections to the change has to this day made no attempt to
excuse or explain or justify its dictatorial parsimony. It
is a case of "take it and like it!" — an attitude to customers and consumers very widely found in Québec and
doubtless elsewhere. We are to accept what's on offer,
never mind that it isn't what we want. In the same way,
when Hydro-Québec noted a sharp decline in demand for
its services some years ago, the utility reacted *by rais-
ing its charges*, thus violating a fundamental principle
of human behaviour. If you are selling something and
your potential buyers make it clear that they don't want
your product or service at your price, you *lower the price*,
and improve your service or product, hoping to make
it more attractive. Not Hydro-Québec! You'll damn well
take what's offered at a price bearing no relation to existing demand. That isn't creeping fascism, that's galloping
fascism, and I can hear the hoofbeats growing louder and
coming nearer, but hey, what do I know?

8

We can't blame our supine posture on a desiccated class system like the dreadful apparatus the Brits are saddled with. There are plenty of loud protesting voices in Britain to offset the tomfooleries of the élites. A TV show like "Yes, Minister," brilliant and perceptive as it is, gives the proof that nobody in Britain is exempt from aggressive, hostile criticism. And look at what's taking place in central and eastern Europe, where one heavily armed and policed regime after another has been set aside by courageous mass revolt. It may be that some of these states will fail to find their way to a truly free political system, but the will seems to be there, and the strong popular organizations for action, often steered by persons with overt and deeply cherished religious convictions, priests and trade-union leaders.

Do we have the will and the commitment to real, genuine, rooted personal freedom to get rid of the from-the-top-down domination of our corporate bodies, big governments, grants boards, take-it-or-leave-it marketing men? In many ways Canada is the freest country in the world, but perhaps our freedom is made of fairy gold. Nobody will come and take me away in the night for writing this essay; there are other and subtler penalties I may be subject to: dismissal as a crank and an attention-seeking egoist, refusal to publish what I write about these matters. We have to keep telling ourselves that our magazines and newspapers and broadcasting networks and educational institutions and our government departments are out of our control. I'm supposed to take my orders from the top down like everyone else, and in my mind I always hear the stern admonition of the policeman. We don't want any trouble here!

The Idea of a Canadian Tradition

...a lonely folk, much given to literature. Distrustful of the life of the senses, though with some musical gift. Not endowed with a great painter or sculptor, possessing few remarkable buildings. Politically responsible, even sophisticated, highly receptive to the odd or eccentric personality in public life. Considered dull by foreigners. Subtle. Hard to know. Fascinating.

Hugh Hood in conversation

Some fascinating Canadians: René Lévesque, Wacky Bennett, Mack Sennett, Glenn Gould, Max Aitken, first Baron Beaverbrook, Mazo de la Roche, Mordecai Richler, Alice Munro, Beatrice Lillie, Pierre Trudeau, Marshall McLuhan. These "dull" Canadians, oh my!

Recognize ourselves?

There's no need to be afraid of the word *tradition*. Latin: *trans dare*, "to give across, to hand across," more loosely, "to hand down" — that is, to transmit from one time or generation to another. There's no eternal law of society and human culture that says people are obliged to do this. Could there be a society without any traditions? It's thinkable: it doesn't contradict deep logical necessity. What would such a society be like, a society without a tradition of any sort? It would be one in which nobody did something because somebody had done it in the past. It would be a society without manners, customs, perhaps without morals, or what are vaguely called "values." A society in which every form of behaviour had the permanence of a fad — say, two years. Where now are: break dancing, disco, the conga, the Union Nationale, Mary Quant?

Imagine a society built on fads! The elderly would be driven out of its cities because of their long memories. There would be no visible burial grounds and no archives. Elections would be held monthly for ephemeral offices, fashion commissar, memory censor, spontaneity consultant.

Assuming that is it desirable to have a few traditions lying around, bundled into a single large one, we have next to decide whether all traditions are good and valuable. What about the custom of blood feud among the Hatfields and the McCoys that lasted for at least three generations in Appalachia, or the very similar social pattern chronicled in the *Oresteia* of Aeschylus? Can there be a tradition of unending blood feud and ritual murder, or is such a pattern more correctly described as an obsessive social neurosis? What about the Mafia, *cosa nostra*, "our thing"? What about the unfortunate habit of the German-speaking peoples of involving themselves in central European wars of conquest every so often? Or that French habit of assuming that all the arts are their exclusive possession? What about the traditional trappings of the Christmas festival, the crowded shop windows and the terrifying materialistic greed? Are these traditions or obsessions?

It appears that when we speak of tradition we assume that what is being preserved and transmitted is *worthy* of preservation. Some sort of value, some human conviction about value, is implied. When we go in search of a Canadian tradition, therefore, we are looking for valuable accomplishments or possessions, a favourable geographical situation, functioning social patterns, great single achievements, examples worthy of imitation.

The vehicles by which enshrined traditions are transmitted are the different kinds of written record, history, literature, law, the library and the archive. And to these means of preserving the past we can now add the wonderfully effective modern means of bringing the past vividly and accurately before our senses, at first still photography, then the cinema, the newsreel, and television and home video, the radio and then sound recording on disc or tape. I think at once of the last CBC videotape of Glenn Gould performing the Goldberg Variations, made not very long before Gould died. The technique of visual recording of musical performance achieved a triumph here. We can see the little finger of the pianist's right hand preparing to strike a single note that will come up in the next bar, the finger quivering with independent life as though the player were unconscious of it — as he probably was. Art in the little finger! Seeing it at work is a privilege unavailable in the making of past traditions.

The great Lillian Gish, in the tenth decade of her life, is now actively campaigning across North America for funds to preserve the visual records of the twentieth century, a collection of material unrivalled by the archives of past ages. Imagine seeing a videotape of Caesar addressing the Roman senate!

Which are the visual records of past Canadian experience that have stayed longest in our minds? I think of the Gould videotape, some of the confrontations between Trudeau and Lévesque, Marshall McLuhan as he appeared in *Annie Hall*, some old hockey telecast footage of Maurice Richard, the documentary drama "Glory Enough for All" based on Michael Bliss's account of Dr. Banting's experiments. It's worth noting that these off-the-cuff recollections are all focused on high accomplishments and wide recognition of them by one's fellow citizens.

If we think of our tradition as a collective myth, a people's saving history, what do we exclude as trivial or harmful? What do we accept as necessary and permanent? Do the Quints and Dr. Dafoe remain in our tradition? What about the Musical Ride, or our unlucky jet-fighter squadrons? Or the nasty anti-Semitism that was widely practised in Québec and Ontario during the 1930s? What about transcontinental passenger rail services?

The Quints are out, and so are the Musical Ride, the jet-fighter calamities and the anti-Semitism. Transcontinental passenger rail service seems about to disappear forever. There may come a time when there is no public postal service in Canada. This too may be an instance of a dying tradition. What then remains? What have we inherited or accomplished that is valuable and must absolutely be preserved? We can do without passenger trains if we have to, because we have air service and the passenger car. We can get along without the post office because of fax and the long-distance telephone. Few of us ever write letters now, and those who do approach the drafting of a letter as a perilous, anxious affair.

What stays in?

The Brits have an extraordinary tradition of political good judgement and invention that they seem to have lucked into. The French lead the most intense life of intellectual criticism in the world. The Italians have been great engineers since they were going around calling themselves the Romans. The German-speaking peoples are the dominant power in central Europe. What about us?

I think immediately of seven elements of the Canadian tradition that are wholly inescapable, no matter which of the two official tongues one speaks, and I propose to list them now. They are not the only essential parts of our tradition. We hold some of them in common with other peoples — the Russians, the Italians. But without these ways of existing our history would have been so different that there would never have been a Canada at all.

First of all, *space*! Marshall McLuhan said of the Volkswagen beetle that you didn't drive it, you *wore* it. And you wear Britain and the other European countries. When I'm in Britain it feels like a closely fitting cape around my shoulders. Nobody feels that way about Canada. You can drive south from Ottawa towards Prescott after dark and in certain places be unable to see any electric lights or other signs of human habitation ten miles north of Highway 401. There's nobody there; the country is unpeopled.

I've come west along the north shore of Anticosti in a freighter and studied the vast empty island spread out beautifully in the sun, five hundred people living in a place almost the size of Prince Edward Island, the deer outnumbering the humans by fifty to one. I've flown into Whitehorse and realized as I looked down that there are about thirty-one thousand people living in the Yukon, the enormous and gorgeous territory empty, silent, begging for visitors. Drive north on an ordinary sunny afternoon from Regina to Saskatoon with the fields stretching away on either side of the fine broad highway, and as you near Saskatoon the road swings up east around a knoll above a big lake, brilliant blue beside the pale gold fields like a painting by Magritte, empty, nobody visible, moving. The scene is ghostly, a mixture of fantasy and actuality. Where is everybody?

The neat, clean, quiet little air terminal in Inuvik. A few footsteps echoing along the arrivals corridor. Department of Transport struggling to fill up the country! You could be in Whitehorse or Fredericton; the footsteps sound the same.

The almost undetectible class system. Sometimes I lecture my unfortunate students about this, telling them that there is no upper class in Canada, that therefore they need feel inferior to nobody. That there is nobody for them to look up to and admire or envy — the other side of the egalitarian coin. Imagine looking up to Brian and Mila and Ray and Gerda! Once when I was going on about this one of the students suggested that she might look up to *me*. This took me very much aback because, to paraphrase Groucho, I don't want to belong to any upper class that I might be a member of. For a caste or class system — which we can cheerfully get along without — we've substituted a network of economic opportunities and exclusions, so that some of us get to attend Ridley College (which makes scholarship assistance available for promising *middle-class* applicants, according to its own advertising) or St. John's or Stanislas or King's, while others never get off welfare in three generations. But we can't quite see the class lines, and many of us are deceived into thinking that they are inoperative. We have a class system that doesn't include class responsibility.

Then there is our chilling millennial secular moralism, which is turning before our eyes into anti-humanism in which our species (the only thing we've got going for us) is repudiated by *soi-disant* opinion makers as the worst and most criminal of the animal species on the planet. Hamlet expostulated

> What a piece of work is man! How noble in reason!
> How infinite in faculty! In form and moving how
>   express
> and admirable! In action how like an angel! In
> apprehension how like a God! The beauty of the
>   world!
> The paragon of animals.

Then he went on to remark, "Man delights not me, no, nor woman neither." Which side of the argument was Shakespeare on, do you think? Our secular moralist — Greenpeacer, conservationist, environmentalist — takes no thought of the next world, and is firmly persuaded that the present world is curable, fixable. And it isn't. I don't know whether to include the syndrome in our tradition or to label it an obsessive social neurosis. In any case it is always with us. The Canadian secular moralist wants to allow unlimited access to abortion and to defend animal rights, to achieve full social justice for gay persons and for women and children, to save the rain forest and redeem our eating habits by doing away with animal husbandry and human omnivorism, to banish crime forever, and sickness and the wrongdoings of governments, the errors of doctors and the sanctions against midwifery, to put us on all fours with all other living species, animal or vegetable (carrot rights, onion insurgency), although David Suzuki teaches us that the cockroaches were here before we were and will remain when there are no more humans. In David Suzuki's eyes we are grotesquely inferior to the cockroaches. We are the most murderous, rapacious, damaging of living species. What a piece of work is man! In the years 990, 991, 995, 999 people were proclaiming the same fearful idiocies, and the world went right on after January 1, 1000, as it always had. We are not going to hell on the morning of January 1, 2000, and the millenarian viewers-with-alarm can say to one another, "Never mind, we must get a winner one day."

We Canadians have received and accepted this twaddle with utter humility; other peoples are equipped with superior twaddle-detectors.

We possess with qualified pride a surprisingly extensive and accomplished literature in the two great languages of our society. We are great producers of literature, though we are not very numerous readers. There don't seem to be more than a hundred real bookstores in Canada, where the employees know and love books and will graciously listen to customers' wants, accepting special orders for single copies and informing the buyer promptly when the book comes in. How many full-service bookstores do you know of? When did you last read a new novel or a new book of poetry? I don't mean a Canadian novel — any novel will do. We are a nation of book writers — everybody you know has written a short story or some poems — but not a nation of book buyers and book readers. We have done one or two very curious things with our fine literature. Some misguided persons have asserted that all the good writing in Canada has been done by women. If this were true it would necessarily mean that we possessed a warped and stunted literature, just as if all the best writing had been done by men. Imagine a great literature — Italian, Russian, French — from which writers of either sex had been excluded! In fact about half of the good writing in Canada at the present time is produced by women, just as you'd expect. It is fair to note, however, that most of the serious reading in the country is done by women.

The other absurd claim that we make about our literature is that we have really, genuinely excelled, have outgone the other great literatures, in the minor genre of the short story. Tolstoy, Chekhov, Kipling, Joyce, Hemingway, Flaubert, Maupassant, Kafka, Singer, those mighty Canadians! It would be a poor, warped, stunted, skewed literature that concentrated on the short narrative to the exclusion of the long. Imagine Russian or French or English fiction without the novel! Imagine Canadian literature without the novels of Laurence, Richler and all the others you think of at once.

Supreme excellence in a minor form. A kind of experience and a moral claim almost definitively Canadian.

Next we observe our strangely self-annulling attitude to war and the mechanisms of conquest. We will fight in

any war but our own! The South African War, the First
World War, the Second, the Korean War, U.N. police actions in the Middle East, Cyprus, Suez, but we will not
fight to preserve our Confederation and we all congrat-
ulate ourselves on the righteousness of the principle.
Canadians will never face one another in arms along
the Alberta–British Columbia border, nor will there ever
be a battle of Hawkesbury. For Quebecers, Hawkesbury
is where you go when the provincial liquor stores are
on strike. No Canadian wanted to do battle at Oka in
1990, and the confrontation ended almost one hundred
per cent peaceably. Everybody's battles but your own —
that's the Canadian war record, and one deeply approves
of it, though with an obscure disappointment. We have
no Helen, and none of us would die for her kiss if we had.

Our substitute for martial glory — a noble and long-
suffering surrogate — and our only true contribution to
political science is the federal-provincial conference, our
chief achievement in political culture. Sometimes I think
I'd sooner go to war than attend a federal-provincial
conference, but I know I'm wrong to think so; perhaps
I've allowed a bit of feeling to get mixed into the thinking.

"I sing of federal-provincial conferences and man."
Opening line of the Canadian *Aeneid*.

And lastly, as our ministers used to say in the pulpit,
we come to the newspaper headline, a super-essential bit
of Canadian tradition, which editors across the country
have kept set up in type for a century.

UNITE CANADIENNE MISE EN DANGER!
CANADIAN UNITY IMPERILLED!

The Times of London used to keep the headline TROU-
BLE IN THE BALKANS permanently set in type because
it could be used on any day when nothing much was happening. In the same way CANADIAN UNITY IMPERILLED
is ready for use of any of those days when everything
seems quiet and agreeable, as well as on those rare
bright days when something seems to be happening at

last. For we must never forget that an imperilled unity is first of all a unity! That disunity cannot subsist in and of itself. The idea of the Canadian tradition lies exactly here. As soon as we created our unity, we began to put it in peril. Before the Canadian girl or boy is out of diapers, she or he starts to worry about our two founding cultures. When he or she has arrived at sixty, the Canadian understands that the debate is going to go on going on. The unity underpins the disunity, which has no other place to go.

Our Lost Vienna

*I am only trying to throw light upon one element of
Dorothy's character and intellect. It is this:
her extreme susceptibility to the Danubian
pretension. She always thought, to the day of her
death, that persons from Vienna and Budapest
and their environs were more cultivated and
perceptive than all others. She thought "culture"
either belonged on the Danube or could only be
consecrated there. It was, I suppose, Joseph
Bard who created this misconception, but there is
no doubt that it governed her unconscious to the
very end. She judged Italian, French, or even
English writers by the value given them on the
Danube . . . and every quality to be observed
elsewhere was enhanced if it were found there.*
Vincent Sheean, *Dorothy and Red*

In the 1920s, '30s and '40s, Dorothy Thompson was
probably the most famous American woman, certainly
one of the half-dozen best informed and most influential
living journalists; she had interviewed Hitler, was the
confidante of the Roosevelt clan, wrote a syndicated
column with an enormous daily audience, broadcast

regularly, spoke German idiomatically in any of three or four dialects and knew central Europe intimately. She married her first husband, Josef Bard, in Budapest, and divorced him in Vienna early in 1927. She had felt so strongly about Josef, who was Jewish, that she reproached him after the divorce, saying that he "made her afraid of becoming anti-Semite."

Such feelings might very well have stirred in her in Vienna in 1927. This was the period when the imperial capital suffered from what Billy Wilder, the celebrated writer-director of *Double Indemnity* and *Some Like It Hot*, later described as "the worst anti-Semitism in Europe." Wilder, born in Vienna in 1906, a sometime law student and journalist there, left the city at the end of the twenties to work in films at UFA in Berlin, precisely because of anti-Jewish feeling among the Viennese.

On Thursday evening, July 9, 1927, Miss Thompson was in Berlin. Like Billy Wilder, she was acutely aware of the social differences between Vienna and Berlin. And it was in her Berlin flat, Händelstrasse 8, facing the Tiergarten, that she first entertained the equally famous American novelist Sinclair Lewis, the author of *Main Street* and *Babbitt*, to dinner. It was her thirty-third birthday. Her final divorce decree from the courts in Budapest had arrived a few days before. She was fascinated by her first meeting with Lewis.

Within ten months they were married, in London on May 14, 1928, and they remained married for thirteen years. The protracted sad story of this impossible union is given in their friend Vincent Sheean's remarkable book. How could the lover of Danubian pretensions, who had learned from her first husband the predominance of all things Viennese in human art, science and culture — how could she have united her fortunes to those of the man from Sauk Centre, the chronicler of Gopher Prairie and Zenith, Minnesota?

When I read Sheean's remarks about Dorothy

Thompson's love affair with all things Viennese and Danubian, her sense that no other European, and certainly no North American, culture or civilization could bear comparison with that of the old Dual Monarchy, the civilization of the Hapsburgs, I realized that something had been missing from my own life during its whole long length. I was born just two weeks before Dorothy Thompson married Red Lewis. Never in my lifetime have I enjoyed the understanding of Vienna and its culture that Dorothy Thompson possessed. Vienna, Prague, Budapest have been for most of my generation and our children's generation a fabled mythical lost place, unreachable, certainly charming but radically unreal. The source of *The Merry Widow*, the music of Léhar and Emmerich Kalmann. The place where Bing Crosby went with his little dog to try to sell a phonograph to the emperor, in *The Emperor Waltz*. I've never possessed anything in Vienna. I lost it before it was born.

In the middle of the nineteenth century, Vienna was the principal European capital in matters of art, culture, mental science, land empire, a much more sophisticated city than the artificial capital of the north Germans at Berlin. A city whose women rivalled — and in the eyes of many excelled — those of Paris for elegance, beauty and chic. More powerful militarily than Rome or London, the overlord of Venice and northern Italy, the heir of the thousand-year-old Holy Roman Empire (not holy, Roman, or an empire, said some cynics), a polyglot capital full of Magyars, Croats, Italians, Jews, as well as Austrians, Vienna surpassed both London and Paris — her only competition — as a European capital. If London boasted a seat of world empire by sea and immense political sophistication, Vienna dominated southeastern Europe, a complex of peoples and languages whose fascination and vitality we are once more, in North America in the 1990s, beginning to be aware of. If Paris boasted a preponderance in the visual arts, Vienna was an important centre for art and architecture and could show her unexampled musical tradition: the Viennese classical school and the Strauss family, Lanner, the Viennese waltz! Rome, Madrid, Berlin, St. Petersburg were simply nowhere, if *savoir vivre* was concerned.

Vienna was the classic focal point of three immense political and cultural forces, the southern German-speaking peoples, the Austrians, the Slavic peoples whose territory was perpetually being spied on and overseen by the czars, and the empire of the Ottoman Turks. For many centuries Vienna stood as the eastern bastion against Turkish invasion of central Europe. During the whole of the Middle Ages Hungary had retained its Asiatic character. In 1529 and again in 1683 Vienna herself was placed under siege by Turkish forces. In 1683 the invading Turks actually invaded the suburbs of the city, which was only saved by the arrival of troops under the gallant John III Sobieski, King of Poland. If Vienna had at any time fallen under the onslaught of the Turks, the entire history of modern Europe would have had to be rewritten. None of the other European capitals has had this degree of military importance in the history of the West, not London or Madrid or Rome.

But the upstart north Germans — the Prussian empire — driven by the powerful impulse to unification of the German-speaking peoples, defeated Austria in the Seven Weeks War of 1866, and by so doing assumed the leadership of the most dynamic and powerful people of Europe, as we are finding out once more in the 1990s. After that Vienna began a long, slow decline to the point where for a time the imperial capital seemed a haunted place, a death-obsessed palsied ruin whose former greatness had been forgotten by the English-speaking world, which for most of modern history had been merely a barbarian outpost of European civilization, exactly what it seemed to Dorothy Thompson as late as the 1930s.

By the Treaty of Prague of August 1866, Austria, Bohemia, Tyrol and Salzburg were politically dissevered from the north, the emergent German empire. The Italian possessions were lost; the Magyars and the Czechs were clamouring for self-determination. That ramshackle absurdity, the Dual Monarchy, began its musical-comedy existence as a shaky compromise that reminds us insistently of Québec and the rest of Canada, in which the Austrian emperor was Emperor in Vienna and merely King in Hungary. The Dual Monarchy tottered along for fifty years until it was torn apart by the great events of 1917, and the throne of the Hapsburgs was overturned, as it seemed, forever. At the beginning of the 1990s voices are starting to make themselves heard in Czechoslovakia and Hungary lamenting the loss of the antique splendours of the Hapsburgs, wishing to have them back once more.

When Franz Josef II and his first minister, Count Andrassy, visited Berlin in 1872, they were told in so many words by Bismarck that *Anschlüss* — the union of all the German-speaking peoples of Europe — was a non-starter. What the newly ascendant German empire required of the Dual Monarchy was representation of the virtues of German culture to the east, as far as the Black Sea and the Hellespont. Western Europe could be left to the attention of Germany. In 1879 Bismarck paid a return visit to Vienna and concluded an alliance with Austria by which Germany bound herself to support Austria against any attack from Russia. Austria in return guaranteed support for Germany in the event of a combined attack by Russia and France. The events of August 1914 were thus prepared thirty-five years before the event.

Since the seventeenth century the appropriate role of Vienna in European affairs has been that of warden of the East and interpreter of the aims of the German-speaking peoples to the Slavs and the Magyars and the very mixed citizenry of, say, Romania, a nation in whose affairs Austria-Hungary delighted to intervene for most of the last century. Persons of talent or genius from all of eastern Europe flocked to Vienna, there to make eminent careers for themselves. When the Napoleonic wars came to an end in 1814, where should the great powers meet to establish the peace that lasted until 1914? Where but in Vienna! All Europe sent representatives to this great diplomatic initiative remembered in the history books as the Congress of Vienna, the creator of our world.

Much earlier than that, the son of a poor wheelwright of Rohrau in lower Austria on the Hungarian border was sent to the choir school of St. Stephen's cathedral, Vienna, on account of his inexplicable musical gift. When the child's voice broke and he could no longer carry out his duties as a chorister, about 1748, he was thrown onto the streets of Vienna to eke out a mean living as a street musician and composer of cassations (*gassatim*, street music) until he evolved into the architect of the symphony, the string quartet, the piano trio — Franz Josef Haydn.

Young Mozart, chafing in Salzburg, unhappy at being treated as a middle-level servant, above the footmen and below the court chamberlain, dreamed all the time of Vienna, of the glittering court, of an official appointment in the capital, of success with his operas before the Viennese cognoscenti. History has retained the record of a single exchange between the emperor and the ambitious young musician.

"A great many notes, my dear Mozart!"

"Not one more than is necessary, Sire."

An emperor, the subject of Haydn's Emperor's Hymn, and a Mozart, brought together in a lightning flash of meaning. A century goes by; the political settlements of the Congress of Vienna begin to show signs of fatigue. Bismarck sows the seeds of summer 1914.

In the mid-nineties Sigmund Freud complained that the anti-Semitism of the Viennese academic establishment was keeping him from his well-earned professorship. The Viennese, he was certain, had always persisted in ignoring their most able sons and daughters.

Gustav Mahler, a Jew, became a Roman Catholic at the same time in order to be able to accept the most distinguished musical appointment of the Dual Monarchy, director of the Royal Opera. He then collaborated with Professor Alfred Roller, director of scenic design for the Royal Opera, on a series of magnificent Wagnerian productions, the first two parts of the *Ring* — "Rienzi," "Tristan" — in a collection of orange, purple and grey sets described with immense affection by Bruno Walter in his biography of Mahler.

At precisely this moment Arnold Schönberg, leader of the second Viennese classical school, was mounting on the extreme chromaticism of Wagner and Mahler the corrosive attack that brought him, and Berg and Webern, first to atonality and afterwards to serialism and the characteristic sound of mid-twentieth-century music. Arnold Schönberg, one of the two pillars of musical thought in modern times (the other being Stravinsky), never did win the complete approval of the Viennese. About 1911 he was earning his living as an arranger of operetta scores! Few works of modern music are as peculiarly interesting as Schönberg's arrangements of Viennese waltzes — among them "The Emperor Waltz" — executed at this moment. Viennese music for the lyric stage was the admired model for theatre music everywhere in Europe and America, as the work of, say, Victor Herbert, makes clear.

In 1902 the adolescent Jerome Kern began his career as a composer while temporarily residing in London. His model was Viennese operetta, his admired master and rival, the great Victor Herbert. About 1914 Kern began to move in the direction of a native American form of musical theatre, now known worldwide as musical comedy. Kern was the first great master of American popular music to liberate himself from Viennese models.

Erich Körngold (or von Körngold if you prefer the index of nobility), the stunning musical prodigy of Vienna in 1910, 1911, 1912, chose a career different from either Schönberg's or Kern's. He interested himself early in scoring for film production and made his way to Hollywood where he became the distinguished composer of many film scores, including additional music for Reinhardt's *Midsummer Night's Dream* and the old Errol Flynn vehicle *Captain Blood*. Later, inevitably, he was joined in Hollywood residence by both Schönberg and Kern, a remarkable musical triumvirate. Mahler, Bruno Walter, Weingartner, Schönberg, Jerome Kern, Körngold — Vienna everywhere.

In 1906 and 1907 and finally in 1908 a young man from the Linz district, an aspiring painter and stage designer named Adolf Hitler, visited the capital and finally settled in for a long stay. He had the good fortune to be brought to the notice of Professor Roller of the Royal Opera, who offered to look over some of the youngster's work and advise him about his course of study. Once settled in the city, young Hitler could never make up his mind to present himself in person to Professor Roller. Perhaps he missed his great opportunity. He became instead a frequent concert and opera-goer.

Mahler had left Vienna for New York a few weeks before Hitler took up residence in Vienna. Hitler did not see the great composer-conductor in a performance of his production of *Tristan*, but he attended performances of the production almost once a month over the following five years, in the city of Mahler and Schönberg and Berg and Webern, Körngold, Klimt, Kokoschka, Hofmannsthal, Schnitzler ... Sigmund Freud.

The clouds were gathering around the setting sun. Hitler tried again and again to have his work accepted by the official art academies, meeting with rejection after rejection. At one moment almost penniless, he took up residence at the Mannerheim men's hostel, a well-run institution for social services, where two of his closest friends were Jews, men whom he spoke of for many years with respect, almost affection. At the same time he was becoming inoculated with the virus of "the worst anti-Semitism in Europe" in a city where if you weren't Jewish you were probably more or less anti-Semitic. He remained in the capital for five years, regularly improving his artistic technique, beginning to place some of his work. By 1913 Hitler had become disenchanted with the multicultural polyglot Austrian capital; he considered it a city of mongrels. There were too many Slavs and Jews in Vienna. He had never been given his due there; he wanted to live in a truly *German* city. He went off to Munich in 1913, and another of the sources of twentieth-century history was revealed. The First World War came the following summer, triggered, Hitler saw, by the murderous attack of a Slav upon the heir to the Dual Monarchy.

The next thirty disastrous years left Vienna a humiliated and devastated provincial capital without a hinterland, the city shown in Carol Reed and Graham Greene's extraordinary film *The Third Man.* Perhaps never in film history has the look of a city served so greatly as a means of artistic expression. The enormous Ferris wheel spins, and the cabin containing the principal actors rises to the top of the wheel. Harry Lime (Orson Welles) prepares to make a murderous attack on Holly Martins (Joseph Cotten) But some vagary of feeling persuades him not to kill his friend. The two men return to the ground. Later Harry Lime himself dies of a gunshot wound, a fugitive in the sewers of Vienna.

I've been to Venice, to Florence and Ravenna and Paris,

New Orleans, Port of Spain, Paramaribo. I've been to New York and to Whitehorse. To this day I have never arrived in Vienna.

The War against the Fetus

Any struggle in which 25,000,000 of the enemy die every year certainly merits the name of war. A medical biologist tells us that the human neonate — neutral terminology — has capacities and value identical to those of the newborn chimpanzee, and need be guaranteed no special rights until age two. Then the human child starts to actualize some of its linguistic and cognitive potential. Human eggs, sperm, embryos, fetuses, newborn babies have in their nature no qualities that set them over other animals. This is the root of the matter. Are we inferior to or on all fours with birdlife, the plants, animals, other forms of life? Or are we somehow their superiors, as Alexander Pope wondered:

> *Placed on this isthmus of a middle state,*
> *A begin darkly wise and rudely great.*
>
> *Sole judge of truth, in endless error hurl'd,*
> *The glory, jest, and riddle of the world.*

There is something fearfully paradoxical about humanity, with its infinite aspirations and stinking actualities. The fetus in the womb, at first infinitesimal, than wormlike, then very fishy, seems such a ridiculous, feeble, *little* object that the claims made on its behalf by so many human beings — that it is noble, the lord of creation — can only be supported by an enormous religious assertion. The question about the value of the fetus is ultimately a religious question and can be nothing else for Jews and Christians. Christ, the God-man, was at first infinitesimal in the womb, then wormlike, then very fishy. He had a human nature exactly like our own in every respect except that of His sinlessness. It is Christ who persuades us of the infinite value of the fetus, egg and sperm.

At present we find in North America two distinct bodies of opinion about the value and right to life of the human fetus. They don't need to be labelled; everybody knows who they are and what they think.

One side holds that the life of the fetus is fully human in its actual and potential states from the moment of conception, that therefore the fetus must be held to enjoy certain specific legal and ethical rights guaranteed to it by the special value traditionally set upon human nature, held to have been created in the image and likeness of Almighty God. The other side holds that the fetus has no special rights and no human or quasi-human nature, that the human neonate is on the same ground as the newborn chimpanzee. Any decision about the continuance of the life of the fetus must be in the hands not of both its parents but of the woman in whose body an alien growth has lodged itself.

A very striking new interpretation of the nature and life of the fetus argues that it is in fact just what I have called it, an alien growth in the female body, something like a cancer or a tumour, life-threatening. There may be some influence here, in popular mythology, from the extremely graphic representations of invasive creatures from other worlds given in such films as *Alien* and *Aliens*.

The scientific discovery that the fetus has its own genetic code distinct from that of its (willing or unwilling) carrier allows statements that cut either way. The fetus may be seen as already an independent being in its own right because of its distinct genetic identity, or it may be seen as alien to the female body that it has invaded, something to be gotten rid of as quickly as possible because hostile to its enclosing life form. For many spokespersons for the decriminalization of abortion, the fetus seems distinctly a fearful alien presence, unwanted by its host.

This is not exactly the ordinary human notion of motherhood, but it seems to be gaining ground in North America. What journalist twenty-five years ago could have imagined the necessity of mounting a defence of motherhood?

There is a visible enmity to our species embedded in this view. This morning I pick up the paper and read in the letters-to-the-editor columns that humans are not as good as animals. Humans murder, torture, destroy, foul, devastate each other and their fellow species. It is perhaps worth remarking that humans work to preserve their own and other species' lives, that they have created art, science and religion. The human paradox: darkly wise, rudely great.

The nearly fifty-fifty split on the abortion question suggests that the grounds of the debate must now be changed. For only some major shift in opinion can resolve these fundamental differences. We tend to forget that exactly such a major shift in opinion occurred between about 1960 and 1990. Before 1960 abortion was treated as a grave offence against humanity, equivalent to murder. People who induced abortions were known as abortionists and were not treated as benefactors of society. They were liable to prosecution under the Criminal Code of Canada. Some of them were in fact prosecuted and convicted of procuring abortions.

Then the great shift in opinion occurred, at about the time that truly effective birth-control methods became widely available. Abortion began to be seen not as criminal, certainly not as murder of the infant in the womb, but as a positive benefaction to women who for one or another reason found themselves unable to accept their pregnancy. Abortion up to about the twenty-first week in fetal life is now widely accepted as morally permissible. About the twenty-second week the fetus is judged by much medical opinion to be "viable," capable of surviving outside the womb, though even at this late stage some viable fetuses are destroyed each year in Canada.

Ordinarily, however, when the fetus begins to resemble a living baby that has been carried to term, our group sense of human rights intervenes to defend it. Prior to that state, the fetus is thought to possess no claim to human nature. It can assert no rights. It is an object to be preserved or disposed of at the decision of its carrier and her medical advisor.

It is perfectly true that this view is a recent one, formed during the past thirty years, by no means the universal opinion of humankind even now. Many prospective parents everywhere in the world do not hold this view of the fetus. It is widely held in China and Japan and the U.S.S.R., in some parts of western Europe and in North America. But it is certainly not universally held now, nor has it been at any time in the past.

This view of abortion is perhaps best judged as part of a more general shift in opinion in many parts of the world, which might be described as a new anti-humanism. I do not remember a time when our species has been so execrated by so many of its members and so hated. Not so much "the glory, jest, and riddle of the world" as the murdering contemptible being that ranks well below the animals and the plants in the order of existence. The view of humanity is being advanced, precisely, by us humans. It is time to think about this secular anti-humanism, right now, when peaceable solutions to our grievous political discontents seem possible. How can we have managed to put an end to the Cold War, begun to dismantle our arsenal of dreadful weaponry, begun to protect the rain forests and reduce our meat intake, and at the same time remained so worthy of contempt? Why do we hate ourselves so? Why make war against the fetus?

The answer certainly lies near the various hypotheses about our prospective enormous increase in numbers. Some demographers are predicting that the human population of our planet, which now stands at about 5.2 billion, will increase by *a further billion* during the next decade, so that the world's population at the beginning of the new millennium will exceed six billion! Does a mass fear of drowning in a sea of struggling humanity pervade our thinking about conception and human fertility? It seems arguable that some such syndrome does in fact underlie all the discussions over the rights of the fetus and its host. Is there not perhaps a graphic representation of the massive overcrowding of our cities, worldwide famine, the constant pressure of underfed, poorly clothed, unhealthy human bodies against our own that clouds our imaginations and makes us fearful? Aren't we afraid that there won't be enough of anything — water, protein — to go around, so that existence on the planet will lapse into an unending competition for the necessities of life? I think that some such image, the child of bad conscience — the curse of the affluent — is at work everywhere in those parts of the world where the war against the fetus is being waged most vigorously. There is a fear abroad that makes us suspect that soon there will simply not be enough room for all of us. Perhaps we are going to drown in ugly, unwashed, foreign flesh.

The War against the Fetus

The arguments over the rights and wrongs of abortion seem to me to be built up over an untapped well of fantasy-fear, a constant horror at the threat of invasion of our life space by alien beings. The notion that the fetus is a hostile invasive tumour, impinging on its host's autonomy, is very similar in structure as fantasy to the image of masses of invading alien bodies pressing on our own. The abortion debate is no debate. It is an exchange of signals about irrational and unconscious fears, a swapping of fantasies.

Opponents of abortion have their fantasies too. Perhaps I should write *our* fantasies. We have expressed horror at the notion of farming fetuses to provide rare and needful biological material for research and clinical treatment. Some anti-abortionists have alleged that young women athletes have allowed themselves to become pregnant at a specific point such that their body mass and muscle tissue would be improved and toned up during the very early months of pregnancy, improving the athlete's competitive potential. After competing in her event, the athlete procures an abortion, disposing of the fetus, which has only been permitted to exist for the enhancement of the athlete's prospects in competition. This seems to be a mythical or folkloric invention. It may be medically possible, but I don't believe that anybody is doing it or is remotely likely to do it. I would be astounded if an unimpeachable authority were to cite a case.

I would also be astounded if some demographer were to produce proof that the population of the globe will increase by one billion during this decade. Increase-rates by no means remain constant. I suspect that these debates have no foundation in fact, but have instead the pressing persuasive form of myth or folk tale. What we have to do to shift the ground of the debate is to clear away the web of fantasies and inventions on either side and deal with these questions on their verifiable merits. Here are some points for clarification:

What *precisely* is the present population of the world?

What *precisely* is the annual rate of increase of population?

How can these figures be arrived at? What are the convictions of those who circulate them?

Are we *really* doing 25,000,000 abortions annually, for a total of 250,000,000 a decade?

If so, what should we think about the loss of human potential involved in the ending of so many lives?

Can we afford to suffer that loss of human potential?

What is the absolute maximum of persons that the planet can support in modest comfort? How can this be estimated?

If the population of the globe is somewhere over 5.2 billion, how many live births should we hope for annually?

How are present death-rates related to the number of "allowable" annual births?

Most of us don't know the answers to these questions. Most human discussions take place upon insufficient evidence about matters that are obscure and ill defined in an atmosphere of ignorance, fear and superstition; the discussion of abortion is certainly no exception. If world population can be shown to be increasing at the rate of 100,000,000 annually, then the pro-abortion camp may argue that we aren't doing nearly *enough* abortions!

At the present time, in the Montreal General H... aborted pregnancies stand in a relation to succes... deliveries of two and a half to one. Twenty-five hundred abortions to every 1000 live births. An interesting and accurate statistic.

Is that what we really want to do?

If we consistently, everywhere in the world, executed two and a half abortions for every live birth, taking into account the normal adult death-rate, at some time in the not-distant future the world's population would stabilize, then begin to decline sharply. Is this what we want to do? The present government of Québec feels obliged to supply incentives to couples to procreate! Do we hope to produce stable conditions in which an already crowded planet remains at its present population level? Do we propose to continue with a steady rise in numbers towards an untenable and disastrous overcrowding?

Or is this matter really in our own hands? Are we in control of the situation?

I don't know the answer to any of these questions. But I do know that all of them lead us towards the fundamental questions about human life, its worth, its nature, its ultimate constitution. And I hold that human life is sacred and free and made in the image of Almighty God. I don't think that solutions to our terrible difficulties will be found only in worship and prayer. But they won't be found without them.

There is a mysterious, supra-rational aspect to human existence, to history. We go along for half a century assuming that the political arrangements of eastern Europe are unchallengeable. Suddenly in a matter of three months they are mined away from within and collapse like the last sand in the top of the hourglass. The power of religious opinion makes abortion an unthinkable option for many years. Then in a decade it is transformed into an acceptable means of birth control. It seems impossible to show what the free play of causal factors has

these strange transformations. How,
ιn what stages? Who can estimate the
moved Mr. Gorbachev? It is known that
.d at his birth in 1931, fourteen years af-
.ution. Do we really have in hand all the
.ssary to judge the currents and eddies of
ιge? I don't think we do.

, sometimes heard it stated that about
200,0ں,000 human persons could live comfortably on
our planet, without the ever-present danger of destroy-
ing our living place, rendering the planet uninhabitable.
Can this be a correct estimate? Imagine the social ad-
justments that would be necessary to arrive at that
figure, a number smaller than the present population of
the U.S.A., about one-twenty-fifth of our present numbers. What sort of purgative process might effect such
a change? A disastrous global conflict? An outbreak of
famine on the largest scale managed by an international
political authority? This reminds us of our high-school
debate over which of the survivors get to stay in the
overcrowded lifeboat. Of course such a reduction in our
numbers could not possibly be managed by any available human means. Nobody desires it anyway. At least I
hope nobody does.

What are we to do? Are we on the side of life or of
death? Are there really two sides to this matter? Do
we have the wisdom, the counsel, the understanding
and the knowledge to direct world affairs in this or
that direction? I am not persuaded that we do. The
notion of Divine Providence surfaces in my mind as I
meditate about these matters. We do not hold our fate
in our hands. We don't know enough, and we don't
have the power to direct our affairs. What are we to
do? We have in effect to choose between life and death.
The human beings who have lived in the twentieth
century have on the whole favoured death and infertility.
It has been a century of repeated mass murder and

genocide, in Armenia, Burundi, Cambodia, the Ukraine, Ethiopia, in Nagasaki and Hiroshima, in Germany and Poland. Everywhere genocide has been the characteristic political activity of our times. We are the people who do 25,000,000 abortions annually. We have wondered long about the choices that supersede the pleasure principle. Many of us believe that the wish for extinction drives out pleasure, that the condition of death is the right natural state, that life is an ugly tumorous aberration on the heavenly stillness of the absence of life. As for me, I'm for life.

How do I reconcile this commitment with a possible increase in world population that threatens to sink us all in an overabundance of flesh? I can't. I profess no solution, only a naive childlike faith in God and in Divine Providence. I can't spell out a workable practical solution, but I can guess at what is going to happen to us. I think that at some point before the end of the 1990s the rate of population increase will slow drastically. I think the hidden causes that will bring this about are already in place: new occupations, new affluence, changes in human behaviour and education, and something too of the behaviour of the rats in psychological experiments whose habits alter more and more drastically as their maze becomes more crowded and more fearful. In the next century we will colonize Mars and the moon, which will not relieve over-population but will at least backstop the possibility of our accidentally rendering this planet uninhabitable; nice to have a spare. Do you see what I mean? We don't understand what is happening to us and we are in the hands of some mighty force (may the force be with you!) that we do not know.

Cher in Bologna: McLuhan Revisited

*...the most heterogeneous ideas are yoked
by violence together.*

Samuel Johnson on the metaphysical poets

A grey Sunday morning in Ravenna — those mighty tombs, those genial repositories of inspired mosaic quiet and empty under drizzle, nothing to do. We took the noonday train up to Bologna to hell around and stay out of the rain while promenading the colonnaded Via Independencia, past the monument to Pope Alexander VII and the heroic statue of Ugo Bassi, up the gently rising slope of the passageway past the successive offices of luxurious banks and fortified money changers — odd presence in the most socialist of Italian cities. Past the two movie theatres and the tables and sidewalk-level displays of dubious goods, wristwatches, scarves, T-shirts in best Benares cotton, bracelets and chains suitable for costuming questionable sexual experiment, proffered by members of visible minority groups, Africans

Caribbeans, here and there an east Indian, grave in deportment, urgent in sales appeal.

Towards Via Ugo Bassi the afternoon crowds began to thicken, the rain to define itself as more than mist or drizzle, a persistent sifting down of fine spray, blowing in under the arches of the colonnade and streaking the fashionable shop windows, darkening the prevailing terra cotta of the arched interior to a meaty, deep greyish red, the colour perhaps of a gourmet sauce prepared *alla bolognese*. It was like swimming along a river of unravelling pasta, an essentially accurate impression of Bologna under rain. We were now coming to the intersection of Via Independencia and Via Ugo Bassi, the busiest in town, certainly congested on the right side of the roadway under the pink-red-grey cover; some event was developing a hundred metres ahead of us, a rallying enthusiastic crowd. Just after the Second World War this might have been a socialist-minded assembly determined to direct the region along the path of political righteousness. In 1975 it could have been the scene of *brigata rossa* extremism. This Sunday a grander ceremony was in progress, the dedication and opening of the first McDonald's in the Emilia Romagna, perhaps in the whole of Italy. Right here on the northeast corner of roadways sacred to independence and to the heroic monk and apostle of revolution.

Naturally the restaurant was packed, and the heaving mass of humanity we'd sighted in front of us was the tail of the lineup of Bolognese enthusiasts of the higher cuisine, gathered together on this wet Sunday afternoon to be among the very first to sample the delights of the menu that has conquered the world. Terra-cotta arches blended imperceptibly into golden arches. We could see diners already ensconced *in situ* smiling proudly, a little possessively, down on the waiting multitude, and were reminded insistently of the miracle of the loaves and fishes.

"There is a boy here with five burgers and two Big Macs, but what are these among so many?" To the Christian the table of the Eucharist remains the first and greatest of fast-food services.

We had meant to have lunch in some obscure and inexpensive *trattoria* nearby but an occasion like this was something not to be passed by. There was no question of immediate admission to the new emporium, but we thought we might get in later in the afternoon; formation of the lineup seemed to be decelerating slightly. This could be wishful thinking. We decided to kill a couple of hours in a visit to the nearest of the movie theatres a few hundred metres behind us in the direction of the railway station. Familiar faces had smiled down from the display posters; who were the stars? A face of dark tempestuous Italian beauty compelled our eyes. The wording of the display advertising proposed no difficulties. *Stregata della luna*. A glance at the pocket dictionary yielded *stregare*, to bewitch, to enchant, *stregata*, past participle, *della luna*, of or by the moon. *Moonstruck*! Sure, of course, Cher's big hit. And the dark tempestuous beauty of the poster is none other than Sonny Bono's former sidekick, later the surprise star of *Come Back to the Five and Dime, Jimmy Dean, Jimmy Dean*, her makeup modified to emphasize a supposedly Italianate origin. We passed into the almost empty theatre and sat, munching on our Kit-Kats, till the film began, when a series of unpredictable anomalies presented themselves. Cher, briefly a Bono by marriage, often referred to by her colleague in TV performance as "the little goombah," actually began life as Cherilyn Sarkisian, the surname presumably Armenian, meaning "child of Sarkis."

TV producers, notoriously indifferent to specific distinctions of ethnic origin, probably calculated that Cherilyn naturally abbreviated itself to Cher and could be construed as close enough to Italian to make no difference. In her TV avatar, Cher figured as Italian and in *Stregata della luna* she looked as Italian, or Italian-American, as a girl can get. Her dialogue was of course dubbed by an actor who had done an uncommonly efficient job, so that the Italian delivery almost coincided with the star's lip and jaw movements. If Cher were a native speaker of one of the southern-Italian regional dialects, that's what she would sound like.

An American woman of putatively Armenian origin, proposing herself as somebody speaking an Italian dialect that might be Sicilian, though the moving pictures accompanying her dialogue were ostensibly a representation of life in New York. A mixed montage of sight and sound.

Other anomalous connections were not behindhand. The moon rose full and gorgeous over the silhouette of some exotic blue-black city much like the renderings of Gotham City in the early Batman strips. The congregation in the theatre, all six of us, stirred luxuriously and whispered together at the immense creamy round image, preparing to respond to such a tale as might well consecrate a wet Sunday in Bologna to romance. Hugely operatic music filled the loudspeakers, perhaps Puccini but even more Pucciniesque than Puccini. A visit in the most fairy-tale circumstances to Lincoln Center in New York formed a crucial incident in the action.

The breadth of the recorded sound, the brilliance of the images of moonlight, the persistent obscurity and mystery of the other exterior scenes, teased and persuaded the sextet in the darkened auditorium with rapidly alternating estimates of the film's settings. Surely that was a New York street ... and yet it wasn't. It was powerfully reminiscent of some other place, but not a European place; those were never Bologna streets. Cleveland, perhaps? But surely this romantic tale, insistently recalling bits of the *Orlando Furioso*, couldn't conceivably have been set in Cleveland or Buffalo. And yet again, why not? There are plenty of Italians in either place. But it had

to be New York because here we were on the splendid
— if undeniably kitschy — staircase of the famed opera
house. Cher and her lover made their way before our dazzled eyes up the grand staircase into their choice seats.
The music swelled and throbbed ... and suddenly were
were in a little restaurant, constricted and half under-
ground, where waiters edged comically between closely
ranked tables and whispered endearments were many
times magnified by the fiendishly accurate sound recording. Above all this sailed the ambiguous moon. Where
were we?

Cher and her dinner companion emerged from the
tiny crowded restaurant, really more a *trattoria* such as
one might find near the theatre in which we sat, and
made their way slowly along wet shining black streets
and sidewalks in the direction of somebody's family
apartment or flat. A jump cut and we found ourselves
in the apartment interior set, in fact a kitchen, but not
one of those cramped gangways built into contemporary
condos. This was a real kitchen, a big room with an
old-fashioned double sink and a dozen wide kitchen
cupboards, a Frigidaire dating from the late 1940s,
linoleum flooring cracked and split in many places. A
massive spacious wooden kitchen table with at least
eight chairs arranged around it at various angles, as
though the members of a talkative, even quarrelsome,
Italian family had just vacated them, the men headed for
a session of *boccie*, the women bound for a bedroom and
general discussion of pregnancy, its causes and cure.
Pale green walls above chest-high tile. The tile triggered
my shout of recognition.

"I've been in that room!"

The four strangers in the auditorium paid no attention
to this involuntary exclamation.

But I had been there, or in a kitchen that was its twin,
in an apartment located in downtown Toronto somewhere south of Dundas and west of Beverley, Grange

or Sullivan or Huron, in the neighbourhood we used to call "the Grange" because of its proximity to the historic home of Goldwin Smith, later the headquarters of the Art Gallery of Toronto, finally the central block of the buildings forming the Art Gallery of Ontario. "I've been in that room." The interiors for the film had unquestionably, I now realized, been shot in Toronto, somewhere familiar to me and my contemporaries at the university and the Ontario College of Art. Old Toronto a few blocks east or possibly west of lower Spadina Avenue, long since transformed by population movement but present here, now, in Bologna, Toronto passing itself off as Cleveland or New York or fairyland.

Sure enough the final credits acknowledged the activities of production crews in both Toronto and New York. The long chain of associations now connected a pair of Torontonians — ourselves — completely familiar with half of the settings in the film, sitting in an almost empty theatre in Bologna watching a movie largely produced in the old home town (which we had quitted some years before), part of the time representing itself as New York, in which an Armenian-American actor plays a young Italian-American woman, her dialogue dubbed in a distinctive dialect of Italian by some anonymous person. This is a ponderous chain, studded with shocking disjunctions and sudden linkages. It requires a remarkable mental ability to unite what is essentially disparate, "the most heterogeneous ideas yoked by violence together." Yes, indeed. And almost anybody who has grown up in or near one of the centres of film production can perform this extraordinary psychological feat with negligent ease. It is strange that only one serious commentator, Marshall McLuhan, has shown how athletic and wide ranging is the imagination of the well-instructed user of the visual media.

Once when I was watching the 1970s film *The Paper Chase* on TV I received a similar revelation. We are supposed to be in downtown Boston where some students at Harvard Law have rented a small hotel suite in order to isolate themselves and prepare for terrifying exams. We see the elevator bank and the entryway to the newspaper-and-candy-bar kiosk. Perhaps the door to the coffee shop is dimly visible in the background. All at once a woman's voice on the soundtrack, half obscured by other noises, says, "Windsor Arms. Good morning." The producers have borrowed the interior of a well-known Toronto landmark and only a very few people, almost all Torontonians, can participate in this particular instance of cinematic syntax. It is a mental action comparable to having read the more obscure poems of T. S. Eliot as they first appeared, before a generation of commentators had destroyed the possibility of such a pleasurable discovery.

The ability to make discoveries of this kind, to construct new perceptual wholes from very dissimilar elements, has been at the exact centre of twentieth-century artistic experience until the present moment. The foolishly named "postmodern" activity in the arts has not surrendered it, but has insisted on it. When Samuel Johnson described Donne, Marvell, Herrick, Cowley and their school as yoking the most heterogeneous ideas by violence together he was pointing the way to the central aesthetic doctrine of our age, the mental ability that fuses the kitchen in downtown Toronto, the Armenian-Italian-American beauty, her dubbed Italian speech, Lincoln Center, the whole bundle of discrete information, *clustered together in a new thing*.

"The mind of the poet," said Eliot, "is always forming new wholes." She sits at the keyboard while across the street a housewife is spanking her brat. Two men argue on the pavement below; there is a smell of cooking cabbage in her apartment. She thinks about Spinoza. And out of these heterogeneous ideas creates something that is none of them, but is a wholly new structure.

Eliot calls the attention of his readers to the analogy of the catalytic agent platinic oxide, which must be present if two specific elements are to unite in a chemical reaction, which never occurs if the catalyst is absent. After the reaction has taken place, a new compound has been formed that physically resembles neither of the combining elements. The platinic oxide is left unchanged, in an exact analogy with the mind of the poet in creation.

Marshall McLuhan made this process the fundamental point of departure for his theories of communication. The Symbolist poem, the creation of Stéphane Mallarmé or Tristan Corbière or Eliot himself, was exactly this sort of *collage* or paste-up of unrelated elements. Film editing, the art of *montage*, provides a second instance of the process. And when McLuhan scanned the front page of the daily paper, what he saw was a collage that was also a montage, a splicing together of materials that had only contemporaneity as their unifying principle. These are the foundations of contemporary aesthetics, the principles that underlie the parodoic aspect and the formal freedom of the art of the twentieth century. These axioms have never been supplanted or even menaced by "postmodern" architecture, which is a parodying, formally free architecture crammed with references of a satiric nature to the architecture of the past. The important postmodern buildings resemble the music of Mahler and Stravinsky in their guying, teasing, irreverent procedures, and in their affinity for conceptual, theoretical, *literary* argument.

In all this activity there is an essential element that is necessary if the experience is indeed to take place, the fusing and accepting aesthetic intelligence. We must *know how* to form and interpret these chains of interconnection, to enjoy our perception of the disparate and apparently chaotic character of what is being fed into the work of art: the little goombah, the rainy afternoon in Bologna, the blend of terracotta and gold. We have to have the ability to grasp that what is important in the event isn't the swarming variety of its elements but the formal structure of the resultant experience. We have to isolate not the movie star, downtown Toronto, the seductive Italian voice, but the new thing, *the process of fusion* that constitutes the work of art.

Information and communication theory depend on circuitry, the miniaturized transistor, silicon chip, binary number system, all means for yoking heterogeneous ideas together. We came out of the theatre late Sunday afternoon with our minds steeped in that so familiar yet so exotic consciousness that we had witnessed things that had no relationship, no interconnection, synthesized in a new form. Andy Warhol, David Hockney, D. W. Griffith.

Later we sauntered back up the Via Independencia towards McDonald's. In about three-quarters of an hour we were allowed to proceed to the upper storey of the restaurant where we received our food and seated ourselves at a small table next to a window from which we looked down on other aspiring diners. We paused before eating to mutter grace and to inspect the décor. We recalled the McDonald's at King and Dufferin in Toronto, replete with memorabilia from the Canadian National Exhibition sited a few blocks away. Then we remembered the McDonald's in Central Station in Montréal, charmingly decorated with rare photographs of the railways that in the 1890s served exurban commuters, trestle bridges, stationmasters with enormous watches depending from more enormous bellies. McDonald's can command the services of the most astute interior designers in existence. What had they done in Bologna? Just what they had to do! The ceiling of the crowded, squeaky-clean space had been cunningly moulded in plastic to resemble very closely the finely formed arches of the colonnade in the street below, and the identical blush of terra cotta shone in the street and over our heads. It is the perception and apprehension of these analogies that *makes* life, as Henry James wrote to H. G. Wells. James and McLuhan are right. The medium *is* the message.

Memory Games, or,
How to Bring It All Back

Lidster ... Edwardson ... Ryecroft ... Mylar ... I'm trying to remember the surname of somebody who is familiar to students of art history, somebody very influential but I'm not even sure what she — or is it he — is famous for. Pemberton.

No. That's not quite the right rhythm. Goderich? Nope. Wyman? Pinehurst?

The answer will be found, if I can think of it, at the end of this essay.

When you get past fifty-five you find yourself doing this sort of exercise, fishing around in your verbal memory for names of people and places, book titles, the exact choice of word to fit into the context of something you're writing or talking about. Call this verbal recollection and ticket it as one, and only one, aspect of your total complex of mentally stored skills. Stop alarming yourself because you find that this type of recollection is becoming a bit harder than it used to be. It is one of the modes of memory that we use oftenest, perhaps the one most likely to signal an alteration in our ability to remember. Such an alteration is regular, normal, relatively harmless and can be dealt with quite readily by the acquisition of certain calculated methods, the first being the ability to relax, in the certitude that the missing word will "come into your head" very mysteriously as soon as you take the pressure off yourself.

And to tell the truth it isn't all that important for you to bring back that name that's at the edge of consciousness. Lidster. Why Lidster? I can't think of a famous Lidster, though there may be a professional hockey player of that name. Does Lidster sound like the name I'm trying to remember? If I knew that, damn it, I'd have solved the riddle. Is the "d" sound in Lidster the same or much like a similar sound in the forgotten name? I feel as if I'm getting somewhere.

It's worth fixing firmly in our minds that this sort of temporary hesitation never has any life-threatening consequences and doesn't matter a scrap. We aren't collapsing into senile decay; we aren't threatened with the onset of Alzheimer's disease. Nor with psychological dysfunction associated with insufficient flow of blood to the brain. We need not succumb to the propaganda shovelled at us from all sides that insinuates readiness for the scrap-heap for the over-fifties.

Think it over! This type of verbal memory forms an infinitesimal slice out of all you can remember, and most of the rest of what you've treasured up in there can be commanded to appear with instant results. Anything connected, for example, to a rhymed verse or a sequence of numbers. Children aren't taught their multiplication tables anymore, but my contemporaries can recite them up to twelve times twelve, which is as far as Miss O'Connor took us, with the greatest facility. Dirty limericks of the clever comical kind, like the one about the young lady of Exeter/whose beauty made men crane their necks at her. No problem there. As we move into our seventh or eighth decades we can readily remember an immense amount of this sort of stuff, as well as all kinds of other matter that we never conceive as part of memory, the motor skills. How to tie a bow tie, something I personally have never mastered. The short chip-shot onto a rolling green, something else I've never learned, but if I had I don't think I could ever forget it. How to sit a horse or ride a bike. How to make love tenderly. Nobody ever forgets these things. How to type by the touch system. Something else I've never learned, as a matter of fact, nor have I ever forgotten my characteristic mistake at the keyboard, the "a" key too lightly struck. Just imagine what's lodged at the back of your mind, an immense resource. And to deal with trivial lapses of verbal recall we can readily develop all kinds of tactics for stimulating that wonderful, funny, mysterious agency that dredges up single words and short phrases and places them, as we say, "on the tip of my tongue."

We're riding from Bologna to Milan in a shining-clean fancy railway car of the Italian state system. Suddenly I realize that I can't remember the name of the actor who played Bob Newhart's wife in his early, enormously successful comedy series, the one where he's a consulting psychologist in Chicago. I can recall that the character's name was Emily, but I simply can't bring back the actor's real-life name. Usual mournful recital of woes: I'm getting old; I'm frightened of memory loss; I've lived off my memory for fifty years; it's the only interesting thing about me, my extraordinary memory. What'll I do if it goes back on me? My life will be over. Noreen tells me to shut up and look out the window. The landscape is lush, the cities are exquisite ... Modena, Parma; why are all the fences made of cast cement? It must be a plentiful commodity.

"All right!" I say. "Cement is a real Italian thing. Augustus claimed to have found Rome a city of wood and left it a city of marble, but what he really left was a city of cement."

"If you can remember that," says Noreen, "you can remember Bob Newhart's TV wife's name."

"Actually she wasn't his wife; she just played his wife."

"I know that, you fool. Come on, let's put our minds to it."

"I've got the rhythm. It goes da-dum, da-dum, with emphasis on the dum. Da-*dum*. Iambics."

"Who knows from iambics? You see, you do remember."

"Da-*dum* da-*dum*! And I think she had a kind of French-sounding name like Odette or Frechette."

We agree that there was an "ette" in it. Or it might have been an "otte."

"Odette Chochotte?"

"Stop clowning!"

A long silence until, just north of Parma, Noreen exclaims "Suzanne" and in the next instant I say, "Pleshette." The "Suzanne" leads immediately to the "Pleshette," but I couldn't say for certain that the first name gave me the second; our joint recall may have been virtually at the same moment, and the method of prompting memory worked for both of us. Put the item into its context: a television series featuring another actor whose name you're certain of, then a rhythm, the hint of a syllable. Then allow your dark powers to steep the missing aural image in the nourishing stew of recollective play. Remember that you can feel somehow — nobody seems to know exactly how — that you're getting close, as we say. I almost had it ... hold on ... *Suzanne* ... *Pleshette*. Wow!

This cavernous land of the nearly-had-it does not form part of the unconscious as Freud mapped it, and seems to have nothing to do with psychodynamics as the psychoanalytic movement conceives them. But we are far more certain that the tip-of-the-tongue, edge-of-the-mind-back-of-the-head countryside really exists in us than we are about the real existence of the Freudian unconscious. Repression, in the terms of Freudian analysis, is a much more purely hypothetical construct than nearly-had-it country, which operates within us every day without any accompanying consultative apparatus, except perhaps a dominating and consoling wife. A psychologist of great genius might be able to show links between nearly-had-it land and the fictive Freudian unconscious, but no such theorist has yet appeared. The vast ranges of what we call the memory, and think of as a single power, remain unexplored. None of us seems to apprehend the remarkable poetic capacity that lies behind our everyday participation in this power.

Choose a date arbitrarily from your lifetime, not a significant anniversary like your birthdate or marriage date, just some ordinary day when nothing special happened to you. Let's say June 15, 1962. I'm not cheating. I've never researched what happened on that particular date, but I'm working on the premise that *everything* that has ever happened to you, from the moment of conception forward, has been preserved in your marvellous mental archive. Let's establish the historical bearings on that date. Mr. Diefenbaker was prime minister of Canada. President Kennedy had been in office for a year and a half.

Noreen and I had begun permanent residence in Montréal just a bit more than a year before, towards the end of May 1961. We'd been living on Maplewood Avenue, across the street from the University of Montreal, for a full year and I'd written some stories about the district. We'd just bought a Volkswagen van, a brand-new 1962 model, and at the same time I'd bought myself a bicycle for forty-six dollars! A Raleigh three-speed machine that I still use. My first year at the university had just drawn to a close. I was conferring with an editor and a publisher who were about to publish my first book; this was certainly sometime about mid-June. We were getting ready to take our two children to the country in eastern Ontario for a long vacation. Noreen was pregnant again.

See how you can narrow the range of the past down to an area enclosed in a single month! I've gotten this far without consulting any notes or looking up any file of correspondence, or my bank statements or cheque stubs. If I went ahead with this research into my memory I could probably dig up something that happened on that precise date, June 15, 1962, which as it happens was a Friday. I know this because I just consulted a table of moveable feasts and I see that Pentecost Sunday came on June 10 in 1962, the following Friday therefore being June 15. What does one do on the final Friday of springtime in Montreal in the early sixties? The shiny new van and the handsome new bike give me a clue. I'm prepared to bet — and I'm beginning to remember — that we bundled the kids into the van after supper and went for a drive up the autoroute into the countryside north of Montreal, to enjoy the long evening light on one of the longest days of the years. Or else I got on my new bicycle and went for a long evening ride around newly discovered districts of the city.

Now a swarm of buzzing information has started to stream out of the honeycomb of the past and I find myself dazzled by quite detailed recollections ... of the look of the newly leaved trees along De Lorimier Avenue in the late twilight, staircases and balconies softening in outline as the light deepens ... the row houses on streets like Beaudry, Panet, Plessis ... all the material that later evolved into *Around the Mountain*.

Every blessed one of us possesses this same magical endowment. Try the experiment! Go on, pick a date and see what you can do with it. You'll be amazed and perhaps a little scared. You will discover to your surprise that you can vividly remember extremely distant memories, whereas you find it hard to recall what you were doing a week ago. This is a very familiar and rather deceptive pattern. Almost invariably what you remember from the distant past has undergone considerable distortion. When you revisit the summer cottage you went to fifty years ago it is likely to seem much smaller than you remember; it may prove to be in a slightly different location than you've imagined.

But now suppose you've been reading a detective story in which Adam Dalgleish asks a witness to account for her movements between 7:00 p.m. and midnight a week ago. The witness stumbles over her replies, and you tell yourself that anybody ought to remember in precise detail what they were doing a mere seven days ago. You tell yourself, if he were asking me these questions I might have a little bit of trouble recalling my movements, but only at first. You cast your mind back one week, last Tuesday night. Hmmmm.

You're rather dashed to find that the pump takes a goodish bit of priming, and you decide that you can remember events in your infancy better than what happened last Tuesday. This worries you a bit, but as soon as the recent memory cuts in you discover to your relief that you can recreate your movements, what you ate, how you were dressed, who you saw, in immensely greater detail and specificity than any imagining of the distant past. That was the night you went to the movies, because Tuesday is bargain discount night at Cineplex. You saw a new film in which a friend of yours has a starring role. You did not buy any popcorn, nor did you drink a Coke. You took the car and parked several blocks from the theatre, which is located in a somewhat inaccessible complex in the basement of what used to be the Mount Royal Hotel. You had eaten a frozen shepherd's pie for dinner, a new product, and it was absolutely delicious.

Your recreation of the very recent past is invariably in a totally different key, a different "registration" than that of the remote past, perhaps less poetic, but far more accurate and detailed. When you're trying to give yourself an alibi, or just to explain to yourself where you spent all that money (let's see, you had $185 in bills and loonies when you left the house, and forty the next morning), you find that the items in your chain of incidents have a remarkable, visible *connectedness*. You know where you parked, that there are lots of boutiques nearby, that you did some window-shopping, that lots of the shops in the Mount Royal complex were still open for some reason, and *bim* goes a 130 bucks right there in a lingerie shop. Seven for the tickets, and you've still got forty; that's $177. What happened to the other eight? Pizza!

The images you resurrect of the summer cottage in 1940 are much more selective than that, much more poetic. In fifty years, when you recall your first visit to the Egyptian theatre in the Mount Royal complex, you may only envisage that lingerie purchase, and what it led to. But you will see and smell and touch the charming details in a way that won't furnish you with an alibi, just make you shiver with delight.

Memory isn't uniform, a pure raw mode of thought or sensation; it's like extremely rarified circuitry, full of sophisticated switching devices, far more subtle and multi-modal than the most advanced computer memory bank. All a computer can do is count very fast. The human memory is insistently blended into imagination, fantasy and thought in such a way that you can remember what hasn't happened yet but has only been imagined.

Habit, instinct, custom, reflex, learning, the exercise of skill or art and — most important of all — the use of speech are all deeply tinctured by memory and imagination, and cannot be understood or distinguished one from another except as modes of memory. We are what we remember. Even in an amnesiac state the sufferer remembers far more than is forgotten. How to move. No amnesiac forgets how to walk; she walks and talks in her customary style. Style itself, our handwriting, our clothes sense, the way we decorate our rooms so that our living quarters have the stamp of our personality on them — nobody forgets these things unless subject to tumour or other lesion, some grave damage to the brain tissue.

Serious diseases or injury can impair our powers, but the powers remain with us; it is their exercise that is impeded. A stroke victim who learns to communicate by some other means than speech can perfectly well exhibit her characteristic courage, strength of will and sense of humour by signals and responses that take the form of eye blinks or other almost imperceptible movements. The person remains unaltered beneath the superficial trauma.

A skill can fade or falter. Even Gordie Howe had to retire at fifty. Mathematicians are said to do their creative work in their twenties, and their exploitation of their original ideas thereafter. Swimmers and gymnasts peak early, jurists and philosophers late. But the gymnast retains something of the divine physical grace forever, while the jurist requires a long span of experience in order to become what she eventually reveals herself to be, one learned in the law.

Muybridge!

What do you mean, Muybridge? Muybridge who?

That's the name of the person famous in art history whom I was trying to remember when I started to write this essay. Who is Muybridge, you ask? Eadweard Muybridge was the celebrated photographer who first captured an authentic record of horses and human runners in motion, in a series of stilled frames in such a way as to show precisely how a horse's legs move while the animal is in motion, how a human runner approaches a hurdle. Before Muybridge even the greatest painters or sculptors had an inadequate grasp of how a horse's legs actually go. For that simple reason almost all equestrian statues and paintings or drawings of horses in motion showed grievous inaccuracies of form. You can only remember what you've truly experienced. Painters like Picasso and Francis Bacon could study the Muybridge photographs and get the legs right. Could you, this minute, make an accurate line drawing of how the spokes in a bicycle wheel are arranged?

Lidster ... Edwardson ... Ryecroft ... Mylar ... Muybridge! See?

Now if only I could bring back the name of that TV series set in the Yorkshire dales, you know, the one about the vet. It wasn't "To Serve Them All My Days" was it? No. And it wasn't "Man about the House." Just hold on a second, it's right there ... it's on the tip of my tongue....

The Persistence of Romanticism

The attempt to define Romanticism, the Romantic Movement, the Romantic Ideal, is a perilous historiographical enterprise; nobody has succeeded in the venture. The Romantic remains an element of our experience that we can know and use and understand as long as we don't look at it too closely. We do more wisely to act under its impulsion than to name and explain it.

What you hope to get from it .

An apprehension of transcendental, timeless reality that delivers itself through great formal sensory beauty (Beethoven, Wordsworth); an ethical imperative that is invariably trustworthy in its urgings (Kant): an access of confidence in our own decisions and actions and a closely annexed awareness of our possession of unconditional liberty (Bonaparte, Byron); fervent, intense practice of the great arts, leading to the production of masterworks (Schumann, Wagner, J. M. W. Turner); reinterpretation and justification of the corrupt history of humankind (Burke, Hegel); finally a right understanding of the articulation of the tragic and the comic, leading to personal contemplation of the numinous or holy (Kierkegaard, Coleridge).

We need not suppose from these ambitions that Romanticism scorns mathematical or scientific or political and social thought. On the contrary the great Romantics frequently display an active, penetrating understanding of the postulates of pure science, as do Goethe and Coleridge. Important advances in probability theory, in chemistry, astronomy and in practical science and engineering were achieved during the great years of the Romantic Movement in Europe. Technology flourishes and achieves great triumphs at the same time; the beginnings of steam navigation and railway transport, the foundations of the theory of flight are contemporaneous with the best work of Paganini, Chopin or Delacroix.

What you actually get from it.

A desperate tragic or nihilistic realization that the timeless transcendental Being is a fictional construct (Wallace Stevens); profound confusion about the urgings of conscience and the act of valuation, embodied in a corrosive relativism (Freud, Dewey); a flight from liberty and responsibility that is institutionalized as authoritarian ethical positivism (Stalin, Hitler); pessimism concerning the revelatory nature of art and an energetic debunking of the artist's claim to a special wisdom or insight (Jarry, Satie, Tzara); an acceptance of history and society as intrinsically wicked (Rousseau, Heidegger); rejection of the categories of the tragic and comic and denial of all possibility of access to the holy (Camus, Samuel Beckett).

A growing mistrust of science and technology accompanies this "actuality phase" of Romanticism. Discontinuity between our religious and moral convictions, on the one hand, and our social and political competence on the other, seems to leave science without a master or a directing ideal. The scientist becomes the handmaid of the power broker, as in the management of research in weapons technology in this century. Nobel presents the Peace Prizes.

When we examine the history of Romanticism over the past two centuries, we discover a perfectly genuine bipolar or dialectical relationship between apparently opposite impulses. One aspect of Romanticism, the idealizing pursuit of the divine, its "ideality phase," remorselessly propagates an opposed tendency or "actuality phase," a relapse into the infernal. Artists like Alfred Tennyson and especially Baudelaire express both of these phases, often simultaneously, uniting a yearning for ideal beauty to a disenchanted horror of the actual (*Maud*). Here we see literary Romanticism transforming itself into Symbolism, just as the radical political optimism of a Shelley becomes the rather sinister conservatism of his admiring disciple W. B. Yeats.

These opposed impulses need not be psychologically or chronologically successive, and are often found as deep divisions in the creativity of a single artist. The visionary optimist Shelley is perfectly capable of "The Masque of Anarchy." Blake continually proposes the marriage and co-existence as one flesh of Heaven and Hell. A profound disquiet underlies the late, apparently tranquil, works of Mozart. What are we to make of Goya, the superbly comic portraitist with his eye for the ridiculous and pompous and his revelations of the disasters of war?

Aspiration towards an ineffable, perhaps mythical and unhistorical reality, merged with acquiescence in terrifying actuality (the disasters of war, the death camps), has been the history of innumerable artists, philosophers and political theorists in the past two centuries. "The best lack all conviction, while the worst/Are full of passionate intensity/Surely the Second Coming is at hand."

This apprehension of apocalypse in the poetry of Yeats, which I have identified as sinister, is the consequence of a political and social insight of extreme intensity. The quoted lines seem to me the most luminous political utterance in the poetry of our century in the English tongue. "Surely the Second Coming is at hand." In the last decade of the second millennium, humanity's intuition of the imminent end of things implies an act of self-destruction. The fields of Heaven and the death camps dwell in one another. The ravaged earth spins in an atmosphere that grows ever more lethal. Soon there will be ten billion of us, an insupportable number. Surely the Second Coming is at hand! Yeats exhibited his view of history as a series of thousand-year cycles or Great Years. He believed that our era was ending with the end of the second millennium, and in some sense surely he was right.

This is the inner intuition of Hegel's *Phenomenology of the Spirit*, the conviction that a bitter and tragic warfare in the spirit, as equally in the world, moves towards the working-out of absolute purpose, a view he shares with Carlyle and Emerson. Hegel chooses a Trinitarian version of dialectic; more recent theorists have had to make do without the postulation of a transcendent Being. The classical Marxist dialectic is the most celebrated model of social and political biology to have been born out of the Romantic Movement. Marx himself seems as clearly an actor in that movement as Wagner, Darwin or Nietzsche, ready to adopt, for example, the concept of industrialism from the arch-Romantic Carlyle.

Process seems to incarnate a persistently bipolar structure. When a novel third element appears to appear it is immediately absorbed into the furthering of process, whose inner nature has not been transformed. Process remains process; there is no absolute; there is no forward movement to history, economic life or evolutionary biology. The superwoman will not appear. Certainly she has given no indication of her arrival. The Second Coming is not a new happening; we have witnessed it before and will witness it again, and we make no progress towards the City of God.

As the absolute slips from our grasp during these two awful centuries, romanticism in the arts, in political thought and in philosophical and theological speculation transforms itself at first into symbolism and then into Semiotics. Everything means, but nothing means anything. The foundation of reality is pure reductive signification, a signification of no knowable specific thing. Signification for its own sake, tendency without purport. The dualistic Kantian assertion of the radical arbitrariness of the sign now becomes the central preoccupation of Western thought. What we know of and through signs is that they are signs: the signifier is the signified.

The act of dreaming is more real than the purport of the dream. What is significant according to psychoanalytic method is the way in which the dream appears to mean, to be pregnant with suggestion that never proffers command or information. Analysis never tells us what broken teeth, or flying, or passing through narrow gaps in darkness convey to us in dreams. They do not purport; they tend without intention; they are aggregations of symbols. Our deepest life is only accessible through the chains of symbols that we consciously select from our treasury of dreamable pictures. The indecipherable late poetry of Stéphane Mallarmé, a poetry that can only factitiously be made to yield argument or narrative, offers an index to the state of Romantic aspiration halfway through the historical process that has brought us to our present predicament.

Mallarmé is to Wordsworth as Mahler is to Beethoven as Symbolism is to Romanticism, where the first term expresses our immersion in the confusions of actuality, the second our reach for the ideal — two aspects of a single situation. We wonder how the transit from Beethoven to Mahler can have been accomplished in as short a time as eighty years, but Beethoven already contains Mahler in himself as Wagner does Schönberg. The Albert Memorial breeds the Bauhaus. It is as long and as short a journey from Beaux-Arts architecture to Le Corbusier as from Tchaikovsky to Stravinsky. Each term contains its opposite. Our contemporary culture is being poisoned by signifier/signified relationships.

The most often practised mode of artistic action in the past hundred years has been parody, where the conventions of a school or style are taken up and turned inside out, as twentieth-century music and architecture have reversed the procedures of the previous century. If nineteenth-century graphic art is sited in curves and arcs, twentieth-century painting and drawing rejects them and proceeds by angles and straight lines. In a rigorous modernism decoration is to be abandoned. *Decoration*, if you please, which the human eye loves and needs. A hypocritical simplicity replaces it. The human form and the natural world — the subjects of plastic art from the earliest times — have been until the past few years alleged to be useless for painting, drawing or sculpture. What is wanted is the (extremely valuable) art of Brancusi or the much less valuable work of the abstract expressionists. The end of this progression is the art that consists of representations of the act of representation, the picture of the Brillo pad box or the Campbell's Soup can or the dots that we we interpret as a likeness of a comic-strip girl; signalling is the subject. We don't see the girl, we see the dots. *Don't sell the steak, sell the sizzle* ! (Elmer Wheeler).

Parody in its etymological root is simply singing about a song. Greek *para*, around, about; *oide*, a song, from *aedein*, to sing.

But perverse humanity persists in dreaming of a third term to the dialectic, which may enrich and deepen the structure of the existent. This prayerful tendency is so rooted, so persistent in our nature that towards the end of our millennium Jacques Derrida sets out to banish once more from human experience — and this time for good and all — the presence of the unmediated real.

You and I know that we are real only in a derivative, wounded and gravely imperfect way. Our natures are fragmentary, temporal, to all intents and purposes devoid of reality. That is how things are; that is all there is. Being is absent. We will be here tomorrow to go on waiting for Godot. Being, the category that stands under (understands) metaphysics, is as Wallace Stevens thought it to be, the Supreme Fiction, finally incomprehensible, unknowable, beyond existence, deferred, cut off, absent, and we are left with the activity of Meaning as Being. Indeed, Meaning precedes Being. Writing is the first action. In the beginning was not the Word but the word processor, writing.

Ecriture, inscription, signalling, ciphering, semiotics, the analysis of what it is to mean — these are the preoccupations of millennial philosophic and critical thought. Tendency without purport, an arresting phrase. What can it mean, what can it be, the act of meaning without meaning anything? The contemplation of Being was traditionally held to lead on to action; certainly this was the conviction of Plato and Aristotle. Being instructs us, informs us. Western religion and science share this impulse to contemplate Being, to decipher it and to make pragmatic decisions on the basis of our understanding of its physical and metaphysical structures. For the great Islamic mathematicians, algebra was not simply a symbolic game, but *al-jabr*, the reduction of parts to a whole, from *jabara*, to bind together. Algebra was an expression of the unity of everything. We have used it to know the truth about what is, in order to act. That is the postulate of both physics and metaphysics: things mean this or that. They don't just *mean*.

The assertion that Meaning precedes Being and is independent of it probably finds one of its sources in Kant's third critique, where aesthetic judgement is presented as a purely arbitrary "floating" activity, without any link to the empirical world or to the noumena. The Kantian dualism leads us to action very much like painting pictures of the labels on cartons and cans, the Brillo-pad world. Aesthetic valuation operates for its own sake and is notoriously independent of expediency or calculation or prudence. This is perhaps best understood in an examination of the sexual life. We value what we value. We may know nothing about art, but we plainly know what we like. There can be no universally binding imperative in aesthetic judgement, but it can nevertheless be imagined or fantasized about as binding. You can fall in love with anybody. The judgement of taste, in short, prepares us for action but does not lead on to action. "Poetry brings nothing about." Auden.

The expressive power of music may be the model for this self-contained thrust of aesthetic judgement. As music, music brings nothing about, gives us no information about what to do. The cowboy who drew his six-shooter and shot Macbeth during a performance of the play in old Dodge City is seen by us as having misconstrued the nature of aesthetic experience and the meaning of the play. We chuckle over his naiveté while Macbeth bleeds. Aesthetic experience is our model of tendency without purport, and we have become very sophisticated in this respect. We continually feel ourselves *meaning*, inclining towards action like a base runner getting ready to steal, without being equipped to seize the moment and act. We may be caught leaning! We are too knowing to try to scrub our pots and pans with Warhol Brillo pads. Fictive preparation for action, without *doing anything* — this is the principal characteristic of our media-oriented world in which we may be entertained at any hour, often, indeed almost always, by provocative or inflammatory entertainments that resemble commercial announcements, and by commercials that are indistinguishable from brief dramas — the video world.

Desire without satisfaction; tendency without purport, Coors commercials, aesthetic judgement that can never issue in moral decision, signalling. An infantile, onanistic existence as deadly as the light we can observe from distant stars that exploded long ago.

As our present age winds down and we seek evidence of an imminent new birth, or re-naissance, or Third Coming, we are more and more forced to ask ourselves if there is any way out of our situation. Three kinds of behaviour are ordinarily settled on by us as avenues of escape: *ideological* commitment, policy and program; *artistic and aesthetic* entertainment in the world in which everybody will be a rock star for fifteen minutes, and *environmentalist/conservationist* hot-gospelling that tells us what we must do to be saved, proffering a new cult and a media-manufactured salve for conscience. These types of activity at once reveal themselves as the creations of the communications media, which purvey insignificant meaning for its own sake. All three are idolatrous and none will save us.

The environmentalist/conservationist best illustrates the new idolatry, because she or he puts forward the image of the goddess known to us from distant antiquity, Mother Earth, or more simply the Earth. Touch the Earth. Protect the Earth. Serve the Earth. Love the Earth. Eat dirt. The Earth gives all, nurtures all, is the one true good, can preserve us, if only for a short time. Save the Planet! This is a persuasive inversion of the religious view that God saves us. We are now to save the goddess. We are to bend and kneel and prostrate ourselves upon the fecund bosom of our *dea mater*, our only deity, our Mother, who swallows us all in the end.

But "I am the Lord thy God that brought thee out of the land of Egypt into Canaan. Thou shalt not have strange gods before me."

T. S. Eliot called one of his books *After Strange Gods*. Sixty years later we are beginning to have a notion of what he meant. His tendency had genuine purport. He may not have been able to foresee our desperate effort of reflection, but his title accompanies us to the end of the millennium and he draws from us a shocking apprehension of the truth of the three great monotheisms, the superb prayer of Islam: There is no god but God.

History as Myth

We might as well begin with the old chestnut that gave Russell and Moore so much amusement. What do we mean when we say to ourselves or to an audience that the battle of Waterloo took place on June 18, 1815? Logical distinctions and problems of definition entangle us as soon as we consider the matter at all seriously. Do we *mean* when we *say to ourselves*, or only when we address others socially and publicly? Do our thoughts speak to us as though we were an external audience, or do we simply think them? Is thinking the same as meaning or speaking? Does everybody think by means of an imagined, inwardly heard series of words spoken by a voice that may sound like our own or may have a completely impersonal tone? When you, reader, are thinking, what are you doing? Listening to an interior voice that addresses you in formal sentences? Do your thoughts have an accompaniment of musical or natural sounds? Do they sound like your father or mother?

There doesn't seem to be any general agreement among analysts of human mental behaviour about these matters. Let us then accept a crude formulation of the relationship between thought and utterance, just to get on with the discussion, and agree that thinking that the battle of Waterloo took place on June 18, 1815, includes neither more nor less information than saying that it took place. If we tell somebody about this historic event, our statement may be quite securely founded on our inner conviction of its truth. Thinking about it and telling about it may be taken to be identical.

This is a very large assumption and may be wrong, but we can use it as a working hypothesis. Very well, we think that the battle took place and decide to inform others about it. Can we fairly say that we "know" it occurred? How do we know? We weren't present on the battlefield nor were we within sound of the guns. We weren't even born yet. We don't know anybody who witnessed the fight. Nor have any of us ever met anybody whose parents or grandparents saw it at first hand. The chain of direct witness is very tenuous. I can't even recall who first told me about the battle of Waterloo. It was probably a history teacher, most likely a woman, who told me about it in the beginners' course in British history given in the schools of Ontario around 1935. What I know about Waterloo boils down to this: somebody, I can't recollect who, told me sometime in the mid-1930s, maybe in 1935, that the words "the battle of Waterloo took place" had a determinate meaning for her that I might in time come to share if I went on learning history.

All our knowledge of history is subject to the series of criticisms proposed here.

We don't understand how we think, mean and utter.

We don't know how far thinking overlaps with meaning and saying.

We don't know what we mean by a historic event.

What are we doing when we bundle a series of discrete happenings together and call them "the battle of Waterloo"?

We don't know where we got our evidence for the existence of almost any given past event.

Who told you about the battle of Waterloo? Did you trust her?

But ...

We all agree that the battle of Waterloo took place, because if it hadn't, we say, the history of the modern world would have been different. We agree to ignore the objection that the modern world could be as it is upon quite different historic grounds. We are quite unshakably persuaded of this judgement even though we have only a vague recollection that somebody once said to us about fifty-five years ago that ... etc. ... etc.

All statements about the past, even the most recent past, are open to these objections. What was your girlfriend or boyfriend doing at 9:00 last night?

How do you know?

We customarily distinguish between past events that we have witnessed (*our* past, our *personal history*) and events that we have learned about by hearsay or by reading about them or by some other form of study. We assume that our personal history is more verifiable, more likely to be accurate, even *true*, than hearsay or learning. The courts usually allow us to testify to the truth of personal witness but will not normally allow us to place hearsay on the record. But are our personal memories really more trustworthy than our recollection of things said to us about events or facts we haven't witnessed? Our personal memories, we know, are often inaccurate and selective. We know that we had something for dessert last night, but was it fruit or cheese or ice cream or all three?

It was fruit, we remember with relief, and what's more we can almost taste it — the plump pear and the fresh crunchy apple slices. But we realize as we perform this delightful mental action — over which we have considerable control; nobody denies that — that a strong element of imaginative mental reconstruction has coloured the memory of the taste of the apple or pear. Imagining a taste isn't the same as tasting. Otherwise the institution of marriage would have fallen into desuetude long ago. In this sense all acts of memory are inaccurate, not simply those based on hearsay or other secondhand experience. To remember and imagine necessarily distorts experience. Our recollections are neither true nor false as to matters of fact, although they certainly can possess artistic and imaginative coherence, somewhat as a work of art does. Memory, in classical mythology, was the mother of the muses. Poetry and story-telling are the daughters of inaccuracy.

This doesn't mean that poetry and narrative are false, even misleading and corrupting, as Plato is supposed to have thought in old age. They aren't even mutually exclusive; there can be much poetry in a story, and the greatest narratives of our culture are either poems (Homer, Dante, Milton) or veer sharply towards the condition of great poems (Dickens, Dostoevsky, Proust, Hardy). Poetry and narrative are interpenetrative, and are the vehicle of *myth*, the mode of narration that is constitutive of our knowledge of the past.

History may be defined as a poetic narration neither true nor false, which a person or a society composes in order to *account for and justify* the past and explain the present. Everyone possesses her personal myth, an artistic ordering of the manifold of our imagination accepted by us as explaining our actions at this moment. Every group, community, society, nation possesses and makes constant use of its myth.

An Englishman, a Frenchman, a German and a Quebecer are assigned to write brief compositions on the subject of the elephant.

The Englishman writes about "The Elephant and How to Hunt Him."

The Frenchman naturally produces a composition called "The Sex Life of the Elephant."

The German produces "A Transcendental/Reductive Analysis of Any Future Pure Notion of Elephantism."

And the Quebecer writes on "The Elephant and Sovereignty Association."

No member of a group or a society who has once entered fully into acquiescing membership in that body can ever after exist without being touched by its most rooted assumptions, its explanatory myth or history. All history partakes of the nature of the corporately imagined poetic story, such that those who possess it freely and fully are enlightened and justified by it in their moral and ethical convictions. They find extraordinary difficulty in freeing themselves from this historical myth. One seldom meets a reconstructed Quebecer or apostate English gentleman. The consequences of a Jesuit education are notorious, and Nietzschean theology deeply dismays, confounds Nietzsche and ourselves. It is almost impossible to give up such a consoling story if it has once been assented to.

And it is likewise virtually impossible for an outsider, a non-participant in a historical myth, to understand how it appears to an insider. The image of the English Canadian in the French-language fiction of Quebec is grotesquely unlike the English Canadian as he supposes himself to be, and the reverse is also true. The English Canadian's historical myth represents Quebecers with startling inaccuracy. It is impossible to be a fully paid up, card-carrying member of two such groups. That is, we do not participate wholly in the historical sense of themselves of any people not our own; this kind of participation can probably only be achieved in our earliest years. A move to a foreign country undertaken after the age of five or six will always be felt as such, the new country remaining foreign to the uprooted personal consciousness. I know of no case of a person fully formed in her attitudes to her native place who after the age of six has succeeded in changing herself into a totally immersed and committed citizen of a new people.

A Scot cannot become Irish; the characteristics of either group are so strongly marked that the transformation is impossible. Nor can a true citizen of France completely assimilate the attitudes, habits of feeling and taste and thought of a German, Iranian or Chinese. It is a question of profoundly differing socio-historical mythologies that raise impassable barriers among peoples. Notions of race, language, culture and often religion or at least ideology surface in our understanding of ourselves and our place in the world as we pass from infancy to childhood. They will direct our lives to the end. They don't always operate in exactly the same way. Geography for example can unite or divide. The British and Japanese have nothing in common except their geography, the condition of being a group of crowded offshore islands, and their consequent need to export (the British Empire, the Greater East Asia Co-prosperity Sphere). The geographical fact does much to influence the cultures of the two peoples, but not in every respect. In the same way Canada and the United States have certain geographical similarities — the Great Plains, the Rockies, the Great Lakes, oceanic coastlines — but very little else in common except language, and Canadian English diverges from American in many respects, eh?

Historiography, the study of the writing of history, is first of all a deliberate choice of narrative patterns. The facts of geology or astrophysics are continually adapted by historiographers so as to fit a previously determined mythical pattern, usually a narrative concerned with the beginning and end of all things, from genesis, that is, to apocalypse. The narrative chronicles the sources of political legitimacy, the descent of kingship and rule, connecting them with a divine origin. The Emperor Hirohito was in our own time said to be heaven-descended, the Ayatollah Khomeini to be heaven-appointed, Queen

Elizabeth II rules "by the Grace of God." Many of us believe the accession of Pope John Paul II to have been ordered by Providence. I believe this myself.

Mrs. Thatcher and Mr. Reagan were chosen by the people who are in the words of the proverb, *vox dei*. In the myth — for that is what it is — of representative electoral democracy, the voice of the people is *said to be* the voice of God. And if it is, then God help God! The voice of the people has endowed us with some remarkable rulers. Hitler, Roosevelt and Churchill, the three greatest political orators of the century, were coincidentally selected by their peoples during the eight-year period from 1932 to 1940. The voice of the people evidently spoke in diverse tongues in these instances, suiting itself to the pre-existent historical myth of the three peoples concerned.

Free electoral democracy with unlimited adult suffrage, where adulthood is achieved at eighteen, allows about as effective a choice of rulers as can be managed in human society. Yet it depends on a purely fictitious, contrary-to-fact assumption — that three hundred or five hundred women and men can in some inexplicable way express the concerns and interests of twenty or thirty million electors: remarkable shrinkage!

Political science isn't a science at all but an anthology of charming folktales. Our Queen rules by the Grace of God and is crowned in and through a liturgical ceremony of the Church of England. Either she reigns under an act of Divine Providence, a notion that I readily accept, or under no authority at all. And the Queen, bless her, is Queen of Canada while she is on Canadian soil, Queen of New Zealand when there, Queen of Australia in that place. There may be some sense in which she is Queen of Britain, Canada, New Zealand and Australia simultaneously wherever she is in the world, but it is difficult to judge what that sense may be. As monarch she suffers from a peculiar sort of quadruple-personality or double schizophrenia. We ask too much of her.

The legitimacy of any ruler, in political theory, can be traced to some mythical version of Divine Right, a political notion by no means superseded by our present degree of enlightenment. Revolutions are carried out in the name of the people, who incarnate the popular will, the General Will of Rousseau, a transparent disguise for Deity. Why not simply accept God, you ask, as the source of political right, rather than the General Will, a shoddy little godling and a poor substitute for an all-wise, all-merciful Divine Person? Why not indeed, replies G. W. F. Hegel, who readily introduces the Divine Will into political narrative symbolism.

Our most pragmatic, hard-boiled political and social decisions are made possible only when we agree to accept a determinate historical mythology, of administrative legitimacy, of the parentage and descent of our rulers, of the representative character of our institutions. Eleven men agree to accept and endorse the Meech Lake accord on behalf of their electors. According to our current political mythology, these eleven are perfectly within their rights as our chief representatives. They refer the matter to their expert legal advisors; they consult the best-qualified constitutional experts of the day — all except one — on the legality and propriety of the various provisions of the accord. They do their artful best to word the finally published text as cannily as possible so that it will compel other levels of the political structure of the nation to accept it as written. It is as if the accord were graven upon stone tablets enshrining an immutable orthodoxy.

The process of ratification by provincial legislatures begins. Seven legislatures accept and endorse the text very speedily; there appears to be a measure of popular support for the text. But then the process decelerates; objections to the wording and the implications of the accord are ventilated here and there, then more widely. Two premiers refuse to propose ratification of the text to their legislatures, partly because of their own objections, partly because they sense the failure of wide popular opinion to support these proposals.

Now a third premier rescinds a previous ratification executed by his predecessor in office. Polls are taken in profusion. Their findings add to widespread suspicion that the Meech Lake accord genuinely commands the support and assent of the political functionaries of a single province, and the journalists and broadcasters in many parts of the nation. The mass of the people in the other nine provinces and the "territories" of Canada remain uncertain about the worth of the agreement. The Meech Lake accord now falls to the ground, leaving us in our present condition.

In all this debate the central question is the ancient political conundrum: how shall the will of the people, or of Fate, or of the gods, be known? Polling is our contemporary equivalent for examining the guts of healthy chickens for omens, the act of soothsayers and charlatans. "Accurate nineteen times out of twenty with a two-percent, or four-percent, margin for error either way." Guesswork, that is to say. Nobody credits the claims of pollsters to probable infallibility, but their goings-on have consolatory and soothing effects.

And when known, cynics demand, is the will of the people sufficiently wise and just to be allowed to prevail? I think it is, but millions don't. The woods are full of pollsters and publicists and other mythmakers who would propose means to persuade and instruct the people, and show them the right way, something I'd be reluctant to undertake myself. Jeffrey Simpson knows the way and so does Lysiane Gagnon and so does Michael Bliss and so does Lise Bissonnette. But only the people, we must insist in defiance of these prophets, only the poor benighted people voice the will of God or the will of the next thing to it, the will of the electoral majority, fifty per cent of available noses, plus a nostril.

An acceptable historical and/or political myth need not have, and on the whole ought not to have, any basis in experiential fact. We will never know what the will of all the people is concerning the Meech Lake accord. "The people" is a fiction. The General Will is a fiction, the representative process likewise. So is the examination of the entrails of healthy chickens, or polling, as sounding board for the popular voice. We have chosen these myths and must live with them until in some hidden way we evolve others that will be equally fictive in nature. We have somehow confided our political and historical destinies to Angus Reid, to Martin Goldfarb, to SORECAN and to Lucien Bouchard, who now serve roughly the function of the knights who assassinated the Archbishop Thomas at the suggestion of the monarch. "Who will rid me of this troublesome priest?"

We might answer, "Who will rid me of this troublesome Meech?" But we have no myth that allows us to voice the true national will. Perhaps there is no true national will.

Folkways follow myth, and do not create them. The tale we tell ourselves is more powerful than cabinet minister or provincial premier. Queen Elizabeth can be divided into four; Canadians are a tolerant people, free from racial prejudice and class distinction; history moves from thesis through antithesis to synthesis; the Queen's first minister is wise and good and truly representative of the wishes and ambitions of the nation; sovereignty is the aim of the ordinary citizen of Québec.

Sovereignty, rule. Who will rule in a sovereign Québec? How will the General Will be determined? By the machinery of electoral, two-or-three party-democracy? Will there be proportionate representation according to percentage of votes received? What will happen to the lieutenant governor, the baby bonus, the guaranteed income supplement? How will Quebec choose a sovereign? Will her picture appear on the currency? What will the unit of currency be called (a crucial element of a national myth)?

Ten Parizeaus will be equal to one Lévesque. Ten Lévesques will be equal to a Québuck. So far, so good. The Parizeau will be a little round piece in a base metal, the size of a Saint Christopher's medal. The Lévesque will be larger in size, though still not very large, about the dimensions of a quarter. The Québuck will closely resemble the Canadian loonie. But it should not carry the image of the loon; perhaps the moose, *l'orignal*, would be more fitting. Much depends on public acceptance of these images. What relationship will the Québuck bear to the Canadian dollar, or the American dollar for that matter? I would find this difficult to predict; the enabling myth has not yet taken form. Certainly the exchange rate cannot be permitted to be fixed by currency traders outside the nation. Such a process would be unacceptable to the conscience of us Quebecers. You bet it would.

Nobody in Québec or out of it truly understands what sovereignty is or implies at the end of the twentieth century — not Mikhail Gorbachev, not the proud premier of Lithuania or Brian Mulroney. Shall we stand together or stand apart? Or fall apart?

Practical Formalism: Mining the Sentence

Meddle with the syllogism, said Jacques Maritain, and you do damage to human nature. He was right. The syllogism embodies the capacity to make inferences, upon which human civilization rests. It is not the only form of inference, but it was the form first described accurately by logicians, and its history is intertwined with the history of thought itself. I would go a step further than M. Maritain and say that we mustn't meddle with the sentence. Tamper with the sentence and you may damage very gravely our human capacity to think and speak. If the syllogism is the prior form of inference, the sentence is the prior form of thought and speech. Everything we can take in, our sensations, imaginings, fantasies, recollections, everything that we judge by instinct or taste, our concepts, is fed to us by ourselves, in articulated segments that take the form of sentences. Our unconscious life is probably fed to us in sentences rather than in a messy indeterminate manifold. We can only communicate with ourselves, in the recesses of our natures, in sentences, the original unit of experience. The sentence cannot be left to the fumblings of transformational grammarians or linguistics specialists or logicians. It is the common property of humankind, which we must be on our guard to preserve against those who deny it or try to dissolve it into dubious atoms.

Consider the sad example of the athletes, and especially the politicians, who appear on televised interviews, trying to communicate their ideas or imaginings. Very seldom indeed do they show any mastery of the sentence; their conversation is peppered with interjected single words or grunts such as "well," "like," "uh," or short phrases like "y'know." This last phrase has for some speakers become a verbal tic; we often hear speakers on radio or television who repeat it every five or six words, adjusting the position of their heads and necks as they utter it, as though there were some close physical connection between their use of the meaningless words and their nervous systems, as no doubt there is. A curious turning of the head to one side and involuntary bobbing or ducking accompanies the "y'know," suggesting an achieved mental emptiness.

The person who can speak in sentences as well as write them has an ascendancy over her fellows. Eliminate the "like" and the "y'know?" and the "uh" (shuffle, shuffle of embarrassed feet) from your conversation and you will rise high in society, a progress that is still, I trust, a reasonable object of woman's or man's ambition. Nothing promotes personal success like clear, plain thought, speech and writing. "Why should I sell your wheat?" "Just watch me!" Sentences that we may disagree with, uttered by Pierre Elliott Trudeau at different moments in his political career. "The universe is unfolding as it should." "The state has no place in the bedrooms of the nation." You won't forget them.

But now let's see you quote another Canadian political figure.

Writing, utterance, thought are vested in the sentence and can't be carried on without it. Below and behind what we write and speak, our inner experience is given to us sequentially and in due form. Our mental life is almost entirely, so far as it can be grasped or fixed at all, a continuing address to ourselves. We are at once speaker and listener in our inner lives. The stability, purposiveness and coherence of our selves, whether awake or asleep, whether fully conscious, half-conscious or unconscious, is given in the form of address, *speech-to*. Reading is obviously a variation on this process; we examine the written or printed or video-projected word, or the painting or motion picture, and we hear it inwardly as speech. Many of us move our lips silently while scanning, looking or reading, as though we were speaking a text to ourselves. Jacques Derrida is perfectly correct to state that writing precedes speech, in this sense, that our experience is received by us as something to be read, deciphered, a series of sentences. Listening to, apprehending, sentence structures is the fundamental activity of the existing mind. Think of the people who speak to you in dreams. What pithy, gnomic sentences they employ!

"Arise and take ship for Basra! There go to the bazaar and accost the first jeweller you see. Buy the lamp he offers you!"

Consider the information proffered by the words in those little boxes at the edge of comic-strip panels, or in balloons, or simply in obtrusive lettering. "Midnight, Gotham City" "Later." "The Batcave." "Next morning." "Commissioner Gordon's office." And so on until the final "Whap" or "Biff." All these signals deliver themselves as segments of experience, units of thought, sentences.

We were taught as children that "a sentence is a unit of expression that conveys a complete thought or action." Despite the attacks of grammarians or linguists upon this classical statement, it remains largely correct and useful and far less limiting than the alternative definitions sometimes proposed. It tells us that the minimum requirement for a sentence is that it is the expression of somebody's experience. The sentence must first of all be *framed*. And once framed it must portray the action of its *subject*, who performs or undergoes the mental activity or physical action (or both) that is described. The framer of the sentence tells us that somebody does something. Take away its utterer and the sentence doesn't take place. Take away the subject of the sentence, or the action described, and likewise there is no sentence. Even the brief words that deliver exclamations imply both a framer and a subject (who are often identical). "Holy cow!" "Golly!" "Who?" "When?" "Drat!"

"Drat!" spoken by the immortal W. C. Fields embodied not just a subject and an action, but a great world of feeling, a context. Noel Coward's "Very flat, Norfolk!" is the biggest laugh line in *Private Lives*, signalling to actors and audience the rich comic implications of a superb first act.

"The cat sat on the mat." Subject: *the cat.* Predicate: verb, *sat;* indirect object, locative, *on the mat.* Easy. Simple! Many brief utterances appear extremely economical, perhaps even devoid of a visible subject-predicate structure. In these cases we customarily say that the missing elements are "understood" by the writer and his readers or hearers. But this device is purely fictive and probably unnecessary. All that we need to understand is that the primordial element of the sentence is its utterer or framer. Utterances made in sleep, or as automatic reflex responses to shock or surprise, groans, moans, pantings don't count as sentences because they are involuntary. Sometimes it's hard to tell a deliberate exclamation from an involuntary reflex action, one "Drat!" from another. And words delivered by subjects under hypnosis or in drug treatment are probably not sentences, though this is debatable. The freely experiencing utterer or framer is, however, the *sine qua non* of the sentence, which can therefore be seen to be intimately connected to the actuality of human psychology. Parrots and chimpanzees and some other creatures can produce lifelike imitations of the sound of the human voice, but they do not produce sentences properly so-called and they produce no literature. "Want a cracker!" doesn't *mean* "Want a cracker!" It doesn't mean anything, and we tease ourselves by pretending that it does. The only beings that make sentences are humans; we should put aside cant notions that deny this. We honour our humanity in reserving the sentence for our own use.

It is the vehicle of one of the greatest and most humane arts. In the sentence lie immense possibilities of artistic refinement, of imaginative and fantastic play, of purely verbal sport, of drama, fiction, poetry. Don't let parrots and chimpanzees mess about with it!

I should stress once more that the *framer* of the sentence is not invariably or necessarily its grammatical subject. I can perfectly well say, "She went to the grocery store," where the subject of the sentence is a person distinct from myself. Nevertheless the framer of the sentence invariably encloses it within the limits of his experience. In this sense, every sentence has a form like "I say that she went to the grocery store." The purely grammatical distinction among first, second, and third persons dissolves under scrutiny. Every sentence testifies to the witness of its framer and is intimately connected with her moral life. To a great extent our lives *are* what we assert them to be. Our truthfulness embeds our being.

Chaucer's Clerk of Oxenford, "ful of hy sentence," was one who habitually spoke in elevated, grave, generally received moral maxims; he had a standard of perfection constantly in his mouth. Chaucer does not treat him as a hypocrite like the Pardoner, but as a dignified and honourable speaker very familiar with the gems of European moralism. Nowadays when we describe someone as a sententious person, we seem to imply a certain sanctimonious hypocrisy in her attitudes and speech. That isn't how Chaucer thought of sententiousness; perhaps his view of it was more just than our own.

The connection of the beautiful forms of the sentence to the various forms that the culture of the West has taken is very clear. The classical languages and especially Latin possessed a cluster of sentence forms that we have retained the names of, though we may no longer understand or employ the grammar and syntax that they named. Clause, mood, indicative, imperative, subjunctive — the names of grammar are almost all of Latin derivation. We have only recently, within the memories of many now living, begun to divest ourselves of the trappings of Latinate grammar, in education and in our personal expression. We are coincidentally becoming less and less a people of the letter. We read progressively less and less and we write almost nothing. The fax machine may help to correct this trend, allowing as it does the almost instantaneous transmission of our lightest thoughts. I wouldn't bet money on it.

Expression is the dress of thought and still
Appears more decent as more suitable.
Pope

As our grammar and syntax change form, our thoughts and our capacity to verbalize them change, too. Probably the most important shift in the culture of the English-speaking peoples in this century has been our pronounced turning away from the Latinate model of sentence construction towards one that does away with more and more of the syntactical underpinnings of expression. I thought of calling this essay "From Syntaxis to Parataxis, or, Who Cares?" but reflected that my choice of words was certainly derivative and might appear captious. I used to think all the time of the different classifications of sentences — simple, compound, complex, compound-complex. I enjoyed thinking about them, saw in them the richest resources of narrative and poetry and began my adventures as a writer by playing with sentence forms the way other kids played with balls and bats.

"I gave the bottle to the baby." SIMPLE

"I gave the bottle to the baby, and she knew what to do with it." COMPOUND

"I gave the bottle, which was full of milk, to the baby." COMPLEX

"I gave the bottle, which was full of milk, to the baby, and she, without having had the benefit of a training course or educational manual, or anything like that, knew at once and with amazing aptitude, which can only have been instinctual, what to do with it." COMPOUND-COMPLEX

Here we arrive at the frontiers of literature. The thing begins not with the word but with the sentence. In my novel *You Cant Get There from Here* I deliberately inserted an enormously long sentence, which takes up half a page of closely printed type. The text is presented as a revolutionary declaration of insurgency and independence — broadcast by a cruel, illegitimate, racist junta. It begins typically — "Mindful of griefs too weighty to be borne, and in the expectation of eventual justification ... " — and continues in the customary self-serving tone of the interested activist. I won't give the entire passage, but I will just note that even the characters in the novel notice the event.

General Abdelazar said to Mr. Zogliu, "What a sentence!"

"Two hundred and twenty words. It will sound even more impressive in French," said Zogliu!

The rhetoric and style of mob insurgency of course originated in France in 1789 and thereafter. Mr. Zogliu is quite correct to notice that this rhetoric and tone are best delivered by the French tongue. The barricades, *Madame la guillotine*, and the rest of the apparatus of revolutionism should only be described in demotic French because that is where it comes from. In this way, the forms of sentences approved by a culture illustrate better than anything else the beliefs, politics, ethics and moral style of that culture. If this seems to empower and enshrine literature as the chief interpreter of social meaning, the most pragmatically expressive of the arts — even more than music or painting — then let the claim stand, for there may be truth in it.

The great writers of our age have characterized themselves and the societies that give them birth in their employment of sentence form. Dickens, Henry James, Proust, Conrad, Faulkner, Evelyn Waugh, P. G. Wodehouse (an unrivalled master of sentence form) and above all Ernest Hemingway have all exhibited their art for us in the way they form sentences. All these writers seem available for parody. Perhaps serious imitation of their writing is the best way to understand and then to love them. Most of them favour the long, syntactically complex sentence as their principal means of expression, but there are invariably exceptions to these observations. One of Dickens's richest and most *directing* sentences consists of the single word "London." I was so impressed by this little sentence that I virtually plagiarized it for the opening sentence of *Around the Mountain*, which consists of the single word "Snow." Both words are followed by extended passages of scenic descriptions, of particular cities in specific moods; both suggest a prevailing moral climate. *Bleak House* is a much greater work of fiction than *Around the Mountain*, containing and giving birth to the later work in the way peculiar to literature.

We find no one-word sentences in Henry James, and a prevailing comic use of the comma to order the long leisurely periods, rivalled by Proust but by nobody else.

"It was with a, for him, careless regard to appearance, that our poor serious gentleman ..." The commas that enclose "for him" are James's commas, nobody else's. The hesitant qualificatory tone, and the nuanced judgement, are made possible by the commas.

Proust again achieves miracles by his distinctive use of enclosed clauses and other syntactical divagations that owe much to Saint-Simon and to Ruskin, but more to *le petit Marcel* himself. His marvellous parody of the syntax of the brothers Goncourt allows us a view of the salon of M. et Mme Verdurin obtainable in no other way.

These matters have a special interest of their own but more than that, the great changes in an entire society's understanding of the sentence sometimes signal world-shaking events. Western society's understanding of itself and its history has altered so radically since the time of James, Conrad, Proust that it cannot rejoin itself as it was then: the insistence on the simple sentence helps to make our century the century of genocide. When I wrote *You Cant Get There from Here* I had in mind Sinclair Lewis's beautiful title *It Can't Happen Here*.

But it can and it does. You can and you do.

The best way to grasp the magnitude of this evolution is to look briefly at sentences that are long and others that are short. I shall provide only two examples and in considering them will argue that our entire world, manners, morals, science, ethical standards, philosophy, religion, use of language, education changed as sentence forms changed.

By a really extraordinary coincidence these two men attended the same English public school, Dulwich College in South London, at almost the same moment. P. G. Wodehouse was at Dulwich in the very last years of the nineteenth century. Raymond Chandler was there in the very first years of the twentieth. Wodehouse was born in 1881, Chandler in 1888. Despite this close connection, a whole world of thought and expression divides them. It is terrifyingly illuminating to recall that although he was seven years older than his colleague, Wodehouse out-lived Chandler by fifteen years. Chandler died in 1959, Wodehouse in 1974. Their great achievements (they are the two writers in English whom I admire most) are *enclosed* within one another's voices and works, in a way that outgoes individual consciousness. They are the turning voice of the English-speaking world from the beginning of the century until the present time. Here's Wodehouse at his ripest:

> And half an hour later I was toddling up the steps of her residence and being admitted by old Seppings, her butler. Little knowing, as I crossed that threshold, that in about two shakes of a duck's tail I was to become involved in an inbroglio that would test the Wooster soul as it had seldom been tested before. I allude to the sinister affair of Gussie Fink-Nottle, Madeline Bassett, old Pop Bassett, Stiffy Byng, the Rev. H. P. ('Stinker') Pinker, the eighteenth-century cow-creamer and the small brown leather-covered notebook.

Look at the way he leaves out the commas in "small brown leather-covered notebook" to allow the sentence to accelerate at the close. The whole passage is a writer's dream, so overwhelming in its effects that I leave it to you for leisured contemplation.

Now here's Ray Chandler at the top of his form:

> He turned and walked across the floor and out. I watched the door close. I listened to his steps going away down the imitation marble corridor. After a while they got faint, then they got silent. I kept on listening anyway. What for?

These two great writers went to the same school and received a classical education within a year of one another, and see what lies between them!

To get from Totleigh Towers to Marlowe's office in Hollywood, you go from Gussie Fink-Nottle and Madeline Bassett through Hemingway and Hammett to Moose Malloy and Carmen Sternwood and Eddie Mars, and as you travel, the human world turns and changes. The footsteps are silent now. We keep on listening anyway. What for?

What Is the Difference
between Thinking and Feeling?

Somewhere in his conversation or correspondence Pierre Bonnard remarks that drawing is the pure expression of feeling, one's use of colour the product of hard thought, reflection. This judgement from the mouth of a supreme colourist not celebrated for his drawings seems paradoxical at first inspection. Surely Bonnard is giving expression to pure feeling in those hazy atmospheric presentations of non-linear space and ravishing colour. Aren't the late works of Bonnard the most expressive and moving aggregations of exotic colour in the painting of the early twentieth century? Aren't his squiggly little drawings trivial and capricious by comparison?

Bonnard's drawings are the reverse of Old Master draughtsmanship — the meticulous, theoretically justified renderings of Leonardo, with vanishing point, geometrical perspective, accurate representation of three-dimensional space. Bonnard's drawings seem to flow down the arm from the shoulder to the fingers, vibrating with the unique muscular tensions felt by this man and by him alone. His drawings are small sudden thrusts of his hand exactly like handwriting and as distinctive as a personal signature. Here, I think, we see what he meant when he spoke of drawings as the expression of pure feeling. You draw from the body; you have to draw as your nervous system, your muscles, dictate. We notoriously draw ourselves in every portrait or rendering of space that we attempt; this phenomenon is first appreciated in the earliest days of one's progress in the art. Nothing looks more like a Modigliani than Modigliani. James Thurber still perambulates the streets of Columbus, Ohio.

Colour, on the other hand, is based on the most rigorous laws of optics and of physics in general. In experimenting with colour the artist submits himself to the world, the angle of the light, the movement across the canvas of shadow as the day draws in, data yielded by the spectroscope. Everybody's signature is good draughtsmanship and perfectly unique. Most people's colour harmonies are in fact disharmonious or flat. Colour is learned; line is in one's nature. As Bonnard alleges, we feel the draughtsmanly line but have to think out our palette.

Early in *A Dance to the Music of Time*, Anthony Powell makes his narrator observe that "nothing does so much harm to feeling as thinking," and in making the remark the speaker clearly values feeling above thought, adopting the received evaluation. Feeling is very widely held to be *purer* than thinking, more innocent, less conniving. If you can only manage one of the two, better to feel than to think. Since feeling is superior to thought, closer to an achieved personal virtue, we must always be on our guard against allowing the full stream of feeling to be dammed up and silted over by niggling thought. "Be good, sweet maid, and let who will be clever." How hardly shall an intelligent woman or man enter the kingdom. Intellect, reason, reflection, judgement, calculation, even prudence are all to be equated with *cunning*. Feeling is idiotic in the Greek sense of being unique and special to the person who has the feelings — Greek *idios*, one's own, proper to oneself.

The harm done to feeling by thinking can now be seen to be that of submitting the idiotic, what one feels, to the exigencies of the other, the world, society. Feeling is personal, thinking social. Too much thought takes away from pure unimpaired intuitive intensity — from which there can be no appeal — of love or rage or hate or joy or anger. If you're angry, you're angry and that's that.

Most of our mental life is intuitive in the sense that we can neither deny its presence nor appeal from it. In this essay I'm not talking about our sensations, our instincts or our unconscious life. Our sensations are right there before us and we can't think them away. I'm hitting these typewriter keys; my gooseneck lamp leans over the keyboard as usual. I can smell coffee, and in a second I'll take a few sips from the cup beside the typewriter. Sensation.

If I'm bowling down Highway 401 and a passing car cuts in on me too quickly I'll make a defensive movement without reasoning it out; the turn of the steering wheel is instinctual. I want to remain alive. I eat and sleep at regular intervals. I have the usual instincts.

Now and then I'll go to bed perplexed by some problem and wake in the morning to find the solution shining and bright "in my head," as Fred Banting found the famous observation about the pancreatic duct of the dog, rising from bed to scribble something down, moved directly from what Henry James called "the deep well of unconscious cerebration." I'm not puzzled about sensation, instinct, the unconscious. I can see that they work. I'm constantly seeing and smelling and touching things. I can ward off a blow and perform the other instinctive acts.

But often in a review of my writing or in a passage in some book about contemporary Canadian literature, I'll be described as "cerebral," "the most intellectual of

Canadian writers," "learned." To a trained psychologist or epistemologist I must appear like a baby playing with wooden blocks. I don't mind that. I know that some of these matters have preoccupied the best human minds for thousands of years. And I do think that everybody ought to have a shot at serious reflection now and then, or serious feeling or whatever it is, to keep the inside of the head fresh and sweet and well aired out. But I'm not an intellectual or a cerebral person and I'm certainly not "learned." I always walk in darkness and the occasional gleams of light are getting fewer and fainter. Learned, for God's sake!

When one of these reviewers or critics meets me at a reading or a book launching, she always says, "Hey, you're not so smart, are you?" And she's right. Sometimes these commentators tell other people afterwards that I can smile, laugh, be as friendly as they themselves. I have feelings too, I think, but as I look at what I've just written, "I have feelings too, I think," I'm thrown back to my starting point for this essay. Why didn't Descartes write "I feel, therefore I am"? How can I tell a feeling from a thought and why do I want to do so?

Sometimes I lose my temper. I try not to do that. I've managed to get it down to a few times annually. I used to be much angrier than I am now. There may be some instinct for self-preservation at work here because when I lose my temper alarming physical transformations occur. I feel as though the top of my head is about to fly off; the blood vessels in my neck bulge alarmingly; my pulse rate soars and my knees tremble: the classical manifestations of extreme anger. Afterwards I am conscious of terrible guilt for having let myself go like that. This degree of anger is almost the strongest feeling I'm capable of, only paralleled in my experience by the raptures of extreme delight, joy or love, also of infrequent occurrence. Artistic delight, the pleasure of seeing something done as well as human beings can hope to do it, is the most frequent of these pleasures to occur, intimate family relations excepted. Like extreme anger it has a solid base in thought, judgement or conviction. I never get angry arbitrarily. I blow my top at folly or injustice or lack of consideration, never at decency or loyalty. The feelings must rise up from judgement and conviction or they verge on lunacy.

There are other unmistakable signs of feeling, spontaneous laughter or tears, a lump in the throat, shivering. Certain music, even some pretty poor stuff, has an overwhelming power to move us; nobody denies that. Some films like the great De Sica films of the postwar period — *The Bicycle Thief, Umberto D, Miracle in Milan* — are unbearably moving. The closing frames of *City Lights*, which I can't watch without tears. Are these tears, or the uncheckable laughter at some of the scenes in "Fawlty Towers" or "Blackadder," or are they the signs of feelings, or convictions? Is the lump in the throat the sadness itself, or the sign of sadness, or a purely physical reaction to stimulus? Some people call De Sica and Chaplin sentimental; they call the closing frames of *City Lights* sentimental. All right then, what about Lear's speeches over the dead Cordelia? "Thou'lt comes no more/never, never, never, never, never." Or Wordsworth's statement in "Michael" that the sorrowful old shepherd often went up the mountainside to the sheepfold he was trying to build, "and never lifted up a single stone." No tear-jerking there, just a bald reporting of the conditions of human life.

These great passages in literature — Priam begging the body of Hector from Achilles, Count Bezuhov on his deathbed legitimizing Pierre while the greedy relatives scheme and sweat, Mr. Dorrit's last moments on earth — make us *think*. Surely the weight of such moments bears deeply on reason. Surely the greatest writers — Homer, Tolstoy, Wordsworth, Dickens, Proust — proceed in their work from the profoundest wisdom and conviction and experience of human life to the more upwards, open-air, superficial if you like, feelings about action and character, illustrated in narrative of the spirit in action. The Leech-Gatherer, Michael, Mémé de Charlus in old age, Sir Leicester Dedlock after his wife has fled, Rastignac faced with the prospect of Paris — the great persuasive unrollings of fiction. Reason and feeling merge here into illumination, which is neither purely rational nor purely emotional.

It seems to me that the function of the great narratives, from the *Iliad*, and *King Lear*, to *A la recherche du temps perdu*, has been to exemplify, to press on us illustrations of conduct that cause in us fusions of the momentary and the long experienced. Perhaps feeling is at once the point of departure for reflection and the goal towards which reflection, pure thought, tends. You start from feeling and think your way back to it. This would explain the familiar experience in which our understanding of and response to a great work of art are fuller, much more understanding of and sympathetic, in maturity than in youth.

But these unoriginal remarks obscure the issue with which I began this essay, which is simply this: how can we tell feeling from thinking? How do we know when we are doing one or the other? Is everyone's inner life the same in this regard, or do some of us have more powerful feelings than others, instantly recognizable as such? They call me a cerebral person as long as they don't know me. Then they call me foolish and sentimental. I don't mind that, but I wish I knew when I was being too cerebral. How can I tell?

I suspect that what gets mistaken for intellectuality in my case is really a blend of two other elements — a very ready flow of language and a peculiar memory that retains some matters forever and can't retain certain others at all. I can't remember the international phonetic alphabet or the derivation of the equation of the ellipse for even fifteen seconds. But I can bring back with terrifying exactness the text of the story "The Peshawar Despatch" by Keith Orme, which appeared in *Collins' Aircraft Annual* for 1935. Ready talk and lopsided memory shouldn't add up to an appearance of intellectuality, but apparently for some witnesses they do. It's a mistake. Actually I'm a stupid man with a very tender heart and I don't know how to tell a feeling from a thought.

What happens to me in consciousness goes like this: my eyes feed in a series of wonderful colour impressions of enormous complexity that are counterpointed by an equally lovely set of sounds — the sound of these typewriter keys, the cars going by outside, three parrots squawking downstairs, a strong collection of stimuli. Then layered through and over these sights and sounds and touches — after all, I'm sitting on a swivel chair — there's this voice that's always speaking quite audibly in my head. You wouldn't hear it, but I can; it's exactly like the sound of an exterior voice, though I don't suppose it makes any vibrations; it's an imagined voice. As I write these lines they are spoken to me perfectly clearly, and I wonder if everybody else's mental life is sectored out in the same proportions: dazzling sights, continuous mixed sounds, firmly defined touches, together with this virtually uninterrupted imaginary discourse, sometimes in dialogue, more often a monologue spoken to me by me, if you see what I mean. I don't seem to form any concepts; maybe this is why I'm so poor at math.

Thinking for me is talking to myself, most often inwardly but quite often externally. Often late at night when the house is still and Noreen and the birds are asleep and I'm alone finishing up a book or standing out on the veranda listening to the wind I'll declaim sentences or syllables to myself, nonsense words or near-nonsense, mainly for their rhythm. This activity plays a big part in my life; it's some sort of chanting, or rhythmic nervous release, something like the vocalizing

98

infants start to produce towards the beginning of their second year, or again something like musicians' indications of rhythm or a sequence of changes in pitch: *ba ba da ba da ba boodly oodly oodly biddly be ba ba da ba.* That sort of thing.

In the only course in logic that I ever took, the professor spent a lot of time tracing up the stages of sensation and imagination and then, he said, when the senses and feelings and the imagination and instincts had done all that they could do, the primordial act of reason took place, the formation of the concept or general idea; humanity, horseness, the square root of minus two. I can believe — that's all it is, belief, faith — that mathematicians can use notions like infinitesimals or transfinites, but I've never had such an idea in my head. As for "humanity," I don't apprehend it as some invisible quantity held in common by all women and men. It always turns itself into an aspect of some individual's behaviour — Wordsworth's or Jane Austen's.

Horseness, the big invisible horse in the sky, is something I don't trouble myself with. I am ready to believe that the pure abstract idea of the essential horse is held in the mind of Almighty God, otherwise there wouldn't be any horses and nobody would even suspect horses, much less conceive of them. I've never formed a concept of a horse, so far as I can tell. I talk to myself about horses: horses, horses, horses, crazy over horses, horses, horses … and I see them leaping about in fields.

I see that I'm depicting myself as a childlike philosophical naif, but under the joking there's a legitimate concern. The nearest dictionary to hand supplies, as the philosophical definition of *concept*, "a mental image of a thing formed by generalization from particulars, also, an idea of what a thing in general should be." That's no help. How is a general idea different from and derived from an image? I don't know. I suspect that there is some important difference between them but I can't voice it.

The classical English philosophers, Hobbes, Locke and Hume, were resolutely opposed to the notion of the general idea; they didn't believe in *abstract* ideas, invisible, unimagined, soundless, scentless somewhats that operate mysteriously inside us to allow us to make mathematical or philosophical statements. But damn it all, mathematicians do this all the time, and do it well, and I can't. That's denied to me. At the same time, I have the power to find my way through life and have a pretty good time doing it. Am I missing something — a mental limb, as it were?

When I wrote my doctoral thesis in 1954 and 1955, I formed the opinion that the human ability called by some the power to form abstract notions, concepts, was *precisely* the same ability as what others call intense creative imagination. What Saint Thomas Aquinas and many of his contemporaries called the *intellectus agens*, the active intellect, performed the same function as our most illuminated and revelatory imaginative activity. *The illumination is the key*. The active intellect doesn't reject the world and the senses, instinct, image. The active intellect loves these modes of conscious and unconscious knowing. And it loves *things*, and wants to get inside them. I make the metaphor a sexual one quite deliberately; we speak of sexual knowledge with perfect rectitude. When we are making love most devotedly we often find ourselves intoxicated by parallel imaginings as counterpoint to the physical act. "Here I am doing this wonderful thing." Fantasy reinforces flesh.

So no, I don't understand the difference between feeling and thinking, but I'm certain at least of this — that *abstract* is a bad name for the action I'm talking about, because it comes from two Latin words (*ab-trahere*) meaning "to draw away from." Thinking and imagining aren't like that at all. When you're really thinking hard you're penetrating things, getting deeply inside them, under their surface colours. Things are all we have to know, and when we know them we are invariably imagining them.

I haven't had a new idea in thirty-five years.

This subject is too big for me.

Televisic, Dramatic, Cinematic

In the mid-eighties I spotted a review by Jack Kirchhoff in *The Globe and Mail* in which he said that *masculinist* was a much-needed word and that the book he was reviewing used it for the first time in his experience. I sat down straightaway and wrote off to Canada's national newspaper, to the attention of Mr. Kirchhoff, to say that I had used *masculinist* in 1972, in the first draft of *The Swing in the Garden*. It appears in the first printed text from Oberon Press, 1975, at the bottom of page 148: " … freed me from that element of masculinist folly." It's a word that English stands much in need of. I predict a wide use for it and its partner *masculinism*, and I'd be mighty pleased to think that I'd coined a word that ultimately found its way into the dictionary. It's interesting too that whenever I use it, everybody understands what I mean.

Current spoken English is full of holes in its vocabulary. What is the opposite of *deteriorate*? We can say, "He allowed the situation to deteriorate," but we don't seem to have a word for the reverse process. "He" or perhaps more likely "She caused the situation to … " What? Perhaps the right word would be *ameliorate* but we use it in a somewhat different way, as a reflexive verb. A situation ameliorates itself. We may suspect that while we readily make things worse, they only get better by themselves. English usage is hard-headed and alarmingly subtle.

Sometimes a subtle distinction is hanging out there in the blue, just begging to be made by the first person to think of a new word, and baby, have I got one for you! *Televisic*, and remember, you heard it here first, and you can see at once what it means.

When I was at university I used to run into early film buffs here and there, the first people who talked learnedly of the cinema. I used to view them with a disenchanted eye because I thought they were making a mystery or perhaps only a muddle out of something simple and delightful, the movies. When they used the word *cinematic* I would grind my teeth because I thought the neologism affected and meaningless. And they were right and I was wrong, because the cinematic is very remote from the dramatic, especially in the narrow sense of "action capable of being represented in a limited space by living performers." As soon as you think about it you see that the movies can do all kinds of things that cannot be done onstage, at the same time remaining incapable of certain central, valuable dramatic effects.

It's the same with the televisic and television as a medium for the representation of action. As Alvie Singer said about photography in *Annie Hall*, "The appropriate aesthetic categories haven't been established." He could say that equally well this morning about what we are still obliged to call "television drama." Television representation of a narrative action isn't in the least dramatic. It is different in essence: it has a totally different grammar and feel to it.

This isn't just a question of words. We only get around to naming new things when once we have begun to understand them. I think we've lived with the televisic long enough for the appropriate aesthetic categories to be established. The televisic is as distinct from the dramatic and the cinematic as they are from each other.

A dramatic performance must be *live*. The performers must be there in the same space as their audience, who can see all of them from toes to the top of the head. The performance takes place in three-dimensional space at the time it appears to be taking place; it isn't on film or tape. A dramatic performance can therefore vary in pace, quality and effect from one moment to the next; the actors may be in better form tonight than last night. Something can go wrong in the middle of a performance, which the actors can correct without the audience's becoming aware of it. Or the audience may become aware of some lacuna in the middle of a show and help the actors through it by ignoring it; they may tease the actors by giggling at some lapse.

Parts of the set may collapse or bulge alarmingly; the pistol may refuse to go off, or go off too soon in the hands of an unskilled actor. Somebody may forget his or her lines, or speak a line too soon in the action, causing a company to omit a large part of its dialogue, then reinsert it accidentally, then play a huge chunk of dialogue over again without the audience's paying the smallest attention. The notion of dramatic performance, in short, is defined by its live, actual state of existence, of being subject to accident and causality in the same space-time location as the audience.

This implies that the focal point of any performance and the number of the actors are limited in size. The playing area cannot exceed in size the proportions of a smallish sports auditorium. Anything enacted in a larger space turns at once into pageant or circus. And the size of a theatrical company is limited to the number of players who can move effectively in a space of limited size. The usual number of actors in a theatrical company need not exceed twenty. The staging must be focused around a playing area in which no more than twenty at most, and usually a much smaller number, may appear at a given moment. The buildings in which dramatic performances are given, or the open-air theatres like that at Epidaurus, need not be monumental affairs. There is a rigorous psychological limit on what an audience of the appropriate size can pay attention to: such an audience should not exceed, say, 750 or thereabouts. The economics of theatrical production are always straitened because of this particular limitation.

If the dramatic is to remain genuinely dramatic it must conform to these natural limitations. That is, it must take place in a somewhat constricted space; there must be a limit to the number of players visible at a given time; the performance must be a live one, open to the perils that all spontaneous performance must endure: forgetfulness, mistake, physical collapse, equally remaining subject to the possibility of an unlooked-for superlative performance or an inspired ad-lib.

It is this condition of actuality that makes the drama so vivid and so engaging in its particular way, disallowing at the same time certain effects that the cinema readily achieves. Enormously wide or high spaces can't be represented onstage nor, therefore, can great military or naval engagements. Think of the difference between battles represented on the stage and those in *The Birth of a Nation*. You can't credibly bring steamships or motor cars or locomotives on the stage. Films are the place for cars, trains and planes. The cinema is vested in mechanical motion, and could not have existed without it.

If there had been no such thing as erotic love, lyric poets would have had to invent it, for the lyric cannot begin to exist apart from the celebration of love. In the same way, if there had been no steam locomotives with big pistons and drive wheels beside which to position the camera, the movies could not have existed as they do. Measurable rotary *motion* is buried deep, deep in the grammar of the cinema, in its unconscious, so to speak. The cinematic effect, moving pictures, cannot be obtained without accurately timed regular rotary motion, that of the film as it moves from reel to reel through the projector. This kind of motion embeds itself in the narrative contents of the picture.

The medium close shot that shows the great wheels of a steam locomotive as they begin to rotate, and the powerfully thrusting pistons that impel the wheels, accompanied on the soundtrack (if there is one) by a "whump ... whump ... whump" as the engine begins to move — this shot is the key expression of the unconscious self-awareness of the movies, which would not have developed as they have without it.

Think of all those rotating mechanical devices, of all those curvilinear motions, by which the cinema lives. Airplane propellers being activated, then spinning at a rate that makes them appear like three or four fanlike filmy webs, then settling into the circular form of the propeller turning at revved-up speed. Locomotive wheels roaring past the camera setup, around a curve, as the words Spokane, San Francisco, Tulsa, Buffalo, appear ... Judy and Gene off on their first vaudeville tour "on the circuit." Paddlewheels on Mississippi steamers, sidewheelers or sternwheelers, and cars, cars, cars.

The silent movies were born simultaneously with the automobile, and have lived on cars. Cars full of Keystone Kops buzzing along the interurban lines of West Hollywood. Laurel and Hardy wrestling with the wheel of an out-of-control touring car. The car as moving plastic object is only less popular in films, silent or talkie, then the locomotive. *The Great Train Robbery. Strangers on a Train. Lady on a Train. Silver Streak. The General.* All about the big choo-choo. Alfred Hitchcock was drunk with trains. *The Thirty-nine Steps, The Lady Vanishes, Shadow of a Doubt, Strangers on a Train, North by Northwest* all contain crucial sequences involving the characteristic qualities of motion that the cinematic effect exacts, the rolling regular rhythmic rotation of high-powered wheels. *Last Train from Berlin, Night Train to Munich.* The visual possibilities are inexhaustible.

The cinema is the visual narrative medium especially and peculiarly linked to wheeling motion. The stage-coach wheels that appear to rotate backwards because of the stroboscopic effect. The twist of the wrenches that Chaplin gives to every object on the assembly line at the beginning of *Modern Times*. Later in the film the machine swallows the man in an arresting display of the medium's inner nature. The cinema and the cinematic are the product of industrial society, the great art of that society. Industrialism exists by means of the lubricated, freely rotating wheel, the linking belt, the shaft and the piston — the engine or machine. These are the favoured cult objects of the great artistic invention of the industrial world.

You see a huge printing press spewing out a long, flipping line of folded newspapers, which slide downwards across the screen on top of each other. Cut to: a bundle of newspapers wired together in a pile, flung from a truck to the sidewalk in front of a newsstand. News vendor opens bundle. We see the staring headline, "D.A. Calls for Conviction." We see the newspaper spinning rapidly, then see successive headlines, "Morrissey Convicted," "Morrissey Appeal Denied," "Morrissey Dies Tonight." Pure cinema.

In all of this, spoken dialogue and the musical accompaniment are purely incidental. The silents were the quintessential films, telling their story by purely graphic means. The cinema differs from both drama and the televisic by being at its root a plastic medium like painting or drawing, interesting because of how it looks. It is scarcely a narrative medium at all.

The televisic effect is something else again. All those lovely cinematic locomotives and cars racing towards level crossings, the people dangling from rope ladders suspended from airplanes have to go by the boards on television. Certainly they can be shown on TV, but films made for the big screen in the golden age of the movies (already a long time in the past) simply don't come across on the small screen in the recreation room, which is far too constricted to deliver the movies' characteristic wide spaces and high skies. Cowboy movies die on TV.

Nowadays theatre screens more and more resemble your recreation-room TV screen in their dimensions; the temptation is for film producers to try to make their product as much like home TV as possible. But who will then pay to watch it? And what then becomes of McLuhan's shrewd observation of the fundamental difference between screen and television images? The projected screen image has its own specific visual texture — flecked, grainy, often rather fuzzy; the television image, transmitted electronically, is "made up" by the viewer and faintly, slightly curved at its edges and immediately distinguishable as itself. Certainly commercial films try to imitate the best, most expensive television commercials, the beer and soft-drink ads.

But the cinema will destroy itself by approximating the visual norms of TV, and will not drive out the specifically televisic effect that is valuable, unmistakable and visually quite unlike the cinematic. In films the deliberately composed musical accompaniment and much of the dialogue are inessential; the quiet natural sounds of the whistling wind or of birdsong suffice. In televisic narration, even though your TV set's sound equipment may be of inferior quality, the sound of clearly understood dialogue is of the first importance. Sir Humphrey and Jim Hacker face one another across the ministerial desk. They bat dialogue across that desk, sometimes for as long as three minutes, an effect unattainable on the stage or screen. Exchanges of dialogue may go on for that long on the stage, but not between two people who do not move from their first position. When Sir Humphrey concludes the exchange with his formulaic "Yes, Minister," whether he has won the exchange or lost it, we have witnessed a remarkable feat of television acting that is pure, essential television. Perhaps better than any other couple, Jim Hacker and Sir Humphrey Appleby have defined in their exchanges precisely what the televisic effect is.

You and your husband or wife are sitting in a normally lighted room in your house, not in a movie house with a beam of light crossing overhead, not in a theatre with eight hundred other playgoers. There may be one or two other people present, not usually more. You are side by side at a short distance from each other; you perceive each other's head and shoulders as life size. The actors aren't twenty feet tall, as human figures are on a giant movie screen, and you aren't forty feet away from them, as during the performance of a play.

The televisic effect allows virtually no distance from the action; you are right inside it. Television requires you to sit close to the screen. You recognize that the persons on the screen are not alive and present as stage actors are; they are almost certainly on tape or film. But they *seem the same size as you* and they are no farther away than your husband or wife; the actors' heads and shoulders are on the same scale as your own. When you watch Sir Humphrey and Jim you have the very strong impression that you are right there beside them participating in a conversation with people the same size as you, in a space that is not really the same space you are in, as in the live theatre, but that is closer to you than anything that takes place on a stage. The televisic is a compromise medium, possessing some of the attributes of the stage and film, and this additional aspect of intimate familiarity that neither of the other media possesses.

We are never as moved by the televisic event as by films or the stage. The shiny sheet of the TV screen is too visible, too close to us, for the pain of the theatre or the awe of films to be effected. What the televisic confers is tremendous, low-key intimacy, the impression of actually participating in the discussion. We can be intensely interested by television, but are seldom terrified or shocked by it; it's too low-key. The images are too small in scale to excite awe, the sense of the sublime. Of the three media it is the most domesticated, egalitarian, very *there!* The space defined by the televisic is room sized, never that of an amphitheatre, hippodrome or stage, or the great outdoors of the classical cowboy movies *Cimarron*, *Red River*, *Stagecoach*. You and me and Sir Humphrey and Jim Hacker in the office, with Bernard in very indistinct focus over by the door: that's what's televisic. Instances of that specific effect can be multiplied at will: Ralph and Alice, Sid and Imogene, groups of Bellamys, Forsytes, J.R. and his clan, the Flintstones, family actions, Johnny, Ed. Two or three people talking in a room.

In "The Honeymooners" the room in which Ralph and Alice act out their exchanges is of crucial importance — bare, poor, terribly intimate. Sometimes the interior of a motionless car supplies the compression and proximity of the televisic room, as in the discussions between Alec Guinness as George Smiley and Ian Bannen as Jim Prideaux, in almost unbearable concentration in *Tinker, Tailor* ... You can't get that effect on the stage; the actors are too far away. And when you try for it on the big screen — Bogart and Bacall in *The Big Sleep* — the images of the faces are simply too big, too black and white, too flat to yield the pressure-cooker proximity that the best of the televisic confers. Alec Guinness was born to play George Smiley on TV — the repose, the quiet beautiful voice, a television voice, not a stage voice. He is a remarkable case of an actor whose artistry is perfect for a given medium, coming to that medium after having passed most of his creative life in other areas of the actor's art.

Guinness has the perfectly shaped head for a television actor. It just nicely fits into the nineteen- or twenty-one-inch screen space, and it has that agreeable roundness of form. Maybe the most perfectly human television image known to me. Alastair Cooke has a head of very similar shape and proportions, a nicely rounded head whose form fits into the soft-focus TV image without distracting, craggy sharp edges. So does Leo McKern; so does the wonderful Siobhan Redmond. And that's your televisic effect.

The Intuition of Being:
Morley, Marshall and Me

Tim Struthers of the University of Guelph once suggested to me that he give a graduate course in the English-Canadian Catholic literary tradition. As soon as he said this we both realized that the proposal might be one of those really captivating ideas that persuade as soon as formulated, then on closer examination turn out to be false lights. Is there an English-Canadian Catholic literary tradition? If there is, who belongs to it? I put these questions to Professor Struthers, who was already disappearing in the distance, running hard with the ball as a born course-designer does when developing a bright notion.

"No problem," he said. "There's Morley Callaghan and Marshall McLuhan, and then there's you."

"Sure, fine, granted. But who else?"

Then there was a silence. I don't know for certain that Tim Struthers ever offered that course, but I've been mulling over the idea ever since he first proposed it. Can there be a tradition that consists of three members? The time span was long enough to establish a tradition. Morley began to publish his work about 1923; Marshall flourished as a literary critic, analyst of symbolism and communications theorist from the early forties until the very last day of 1980; and I'm still pretty active and hope to stick around for a while. A tradition extending over most of a century — that's long enough, though not too long, for it to establish itself. But I'm impelled to wonder about the number of its members and possible descendants. Where are the other English-Canadian Catholic fiction writers, poets, dramatists, critics in this tradition? Has it perpetuated itself; will it continue? Do Morley and Marshall and I have enough in common, or enough significance, to earn the continuance of this supposed tradition? I can't name other possible members of such a clan, and I'm not foolish enough to try to create a literary tradition on my own say-so. I'll leave that operation to people like Stan Dragland.

On a first look it seems as though Catholic literary activity in English hasn't made much of a place for itself in North American literature. I think first of the superb Flannery O'Connor, in my opinion the best American fiction writer of the past fifty years. There's Walker Percy, of course, who defines a kind of Catholic existentialism, though he may not have been an assenting dogmatic Catholic. There was Hemingway's brief flirtation with Catholicism, a somewhat longer sojourn in the Faith by Robert Lowell, and the remarkable stopover of Tennessee Williams. None of these last forays caused their perpetrators to be identified as forming some sort of American-Catholic literary tradition. Catholic writing in America seems to be distinguished largely by writers who were Catholics for an inning or two, then concluded that no, this wasn't their final position.

With the best will in the world I can't claim James Joyce as a Catholic writer. Evelyn Waugh and Graham Greene, both convinced Catholic converts, signalled to their readers for decades that they did not care to be read as "Catholic writers." Nor do I.

I don't think that Morley Callaghan and Marshall McLuhan wished to be read as Catholic writers either, certainly not in the sense of making propaganda for the dogmatic minutiae of Catholic belief. But as I reflect on this difficult matter I think I begin to see a bundle of connections linking the three of us, which all have to do with what Jacques Maritain called "the intuition of Being."

Last night on a PBS television show devoted to his extraordinary career I heard John Cage describing the view of the Zen masters, that if you are bored by something for two minutes you ought to go on to contemplate that thing for four minutes, or eight, or sixteen or sixty-four. At the end of a certain time — whether long or short — you will begin to find the object of contemplation hypnotically fascinating. I have invariably found this to be true; it squares perfectly with something I learned during my early religious instruction, that the contemplation of a single object, a rose or a brick or a purple martin, might last a lifetime, because every possible object of thought was sustained in existence by the Divine Reason, Love and Will, that in the words of the ancients, everything is full of God. The intuition of Being, whether fostered by the Zen sage or by the poet William Carlos Williams ("no ideas but in things"), will finally confer a direct apprehension of the preserving and sustaining movement of pure Being in things.

We sometimes misinterpret Williams's statement to mean that there are no ideas at all, but he doesn't say that. He says that ideas are invariably embedded in particular objects. They aren't floating around in a Platonic heaven, freed from the unfortunate condition of flesh. The ideas can only live in the flesh, in the horse or diamond or lump of mud. That's where the ideas are; it's there that the intuition of Being must penetrate.

I think that this conviction is the linking connection between the three of us. Morley Callaghan dedicated his novel *Such Is My Beloved* to "those times with M. in the winter of 1933." The initial M stood for Maritain, with whom Morley had a series of revelatory conversations when the philosopher was living in Toronto and delivering philosophical instruction at the Pontifical Institute of Mediaeval Studies on the campus of Saint Michael's College.

A few years before, Morley had produced a complex novella, "In His Own Country," which appeared in his first story collection *A Native Argosy*, in 1929. In this unusual narrative, a young man living in a lakeside Ontario town something like Collingwood learns of the setting-up of a centre for metaphysical research at the Catholic college of the nearby city university. He becomes fascinated, in near solitude, almost wholly on his own, by what seems to be a natural metaphysical intuition that he himself possesses. He leaves his family to go to the city and discuss this business with the philosophers of the Catholic tradition. Something strange happens to him in the city. He passes through a crisis of revelatory intuition and enters a state of withdrawal.

Sometime later he is picked up on the streets of the city and returned to his home town, where he becomes the ward of his family, his mother and his wife, apparently unable or unwilling to speak. He is clearly aware of what goes on around him but it has no attraction for him. He can smile and nod but remains silent. The title of the novella is highly suggestive. Christ would work no miracle in Nazareth. A prophet is without honour in his own country.

The young amateur philosopher has undergone a release of intelligibility, a profound, perhaps frightening intuition of reality, for which he is unprepared. This leaves him amazed, astounded, captivated by the radiance of pure Being. A strangely persuasive and significant story, typical of Callaghan's insight and intentions. He was from first to last a philosophical novelist, preoccupied with metaphysical and spiritual matters, as his work from *Such Is My Beloved* to *The Loved and the Lost* shows. Significant supporting references to contemporary Catholic philosophical thought can be uncovered in his semi-fictional memoir, *The Varsity Story*, 1948, written and published just when Marshall McLuhan was interesting himself most deeply in the theory of the analogy of Being as propounded by Saint Thomas Aquinas, whose views were at that time being edited as the treatise *De Analogia* by Father Armand Maurer at the Pontifical Institute.

The theory of the analogy of Being, as worked out by the great Scholastics, offers a systematic credible answer to the question put by Saint Thomas, "whether any names may be predicated of God, except analogically." The Thomistic answer to the question is a carefully qualified no. And the long history of this matter is advanced and clarified, but perhaps not concluded there. Since the appearance of the anonymous fifth-century writer known to history as "the pseudo-Dionysius," philosophers, theologians and mystics had debated the propriety of applying human language, humanly conceived names, to the Being of the Almighty. The question remains at the centre of the thought of the contemporary theorist of Absence, Jacques Derrida.

The philosophers and mystics who taught the *via negativa* held that humankind cannot say anything true of God, as the Divine Nature cannot be captured by the categories of human thought. (Wittgenstein: "Whereof one cannot speak, thereof one must be silent.") God is beyond Being and beyond language. The Divine Absolute must be apprehended — if at all — by the mystical way of unknowing, as described for example by the anonymous author of the fourteenth-century treatise *The Cloud of Unknowing*. The school of Rhineland mystics headed by the Dominican Meister Eckhart shows a progression in the mid-fourteenth century towards the adoption of the negative way as our only means of drawing closer to God.

At the end of the previous century, with the aid of a sophisticated logical apparatus, the great Scholastic rationalists had sought a means of explaining how human thought and language might be able to speak of God, not as God knows and contemplates the Divine Essence but by some legitimate, rational, human procedure. The solution of Saint Thomas and his school was the doctrine of the analogy of proportionality. We cannot name God as God is, in Being and Essence, or mathematically, but we can intuit that all that exists is analogous to the Divine Existence, in due proportion to the natures of individual things. The whole of Being is a multiform system of analogical relations in which everything that is possesses a mode of being, and to that degree bears a proportionate analogical relationship to the Almighty. The human person who contemplates Being as such will know it to be a system that unites the purple martin, the diamond and the lump of mud, through the supportive maintaining-in-existence of the presence of God.

It was a blinding insight of this kind that afflicted the hero of the novella "In His Own Country" and left him speechless. Suddenly he saw and knew more than he could take in and comprehend. The unifying element in the tradition represented by Morley, Marshall and me is precisely this sliding scale of analogical relationships, pulsing with significance, the fundamental insight characteristic of McLuhan's thinking around 1948, when all of us at Saint Michael's College were excitedly discussing Father Maurer's work on the treatise *De Analogia*.

I can vividly recall the appearance of Morley's *The Varsity Story* that same year, with its references to the philosophical undertakings of the Basilian fathers at Saint Mike's. Simultaneously Marshall was expressing his great interest in the theory of analogy during the run-up to the publication of *The Mechanical Bride*, 1951.

The title of that famous book proposes an analogical perception. An automobile isn't univocally like a newly married woman, nor is there the punning likeness of equivocation. But yes, there is a true analogical relationship. The good man loves his bride in a certain way, but he may also love his new car in another way; the loves are not exactly alike or of similar value, but they have a certain proportion to one another. The specific and unmistakable McLuhan wit and humour are largely based on analogies of proportion.

I had Marshall as an instructor in several undergraduate courses between 1947 and 1950, in two advanced graduate seminars in the early fifties and in an informal seminar on the great books of modernism ca. 1947: Eisenstein, Mumford, Sorokin, Horney, Moholy-Nagy, Giedion, a galaxy of unfamiliar masters. His critical approach to symbolism, modernism and the works of Joyce, Eliot and Pound now seems to me to have been saturated with analogical understanding, a way of penetrating the structure of existence first revealed in his 1944 article on Gerard Manley Hopkins, "The Analogical Mirrors," which appeared in *The Kenyon Review*. This article, and his seminar-room comments on the system of relationships among all existing things, gave me the same excited awareness that something significant was happening to me that reading Mr. Callaghan's theocentric novels, *Such Is My Beloved*, *More Joy in Heaven* and *The Loved and the Lost*, did in the early 1950s.

Morley's work in this genre everywhere invoked the idea of the fire of the Divine Love. "Many waters cannot quench Love." I found myself bringing together two fundamental notions in Christian thought, the conception of the analogy of Being, and that of the fire of Divine Love. "There lives the dearest freshness deep down things," wrote Hopkins. In this poet I discovered the same shining awareness of the life that pulses in the deepest interior of all individual existents. I could see that this life was conferred by the power of "*l'amor che move il sole a l'altre stelle* ," as Dante says in the closing line of the *Paradiso* .

While I was listening to Marshall in the lecture or seminar room three or four times weekly, about 1950-1953, I found myself working on a doctoral thesis about the theory of the imagination. The further I went with my research, the more I became convinced that the creative imagination and the active illuminating intellect were the same power, an eternizing, revealing power, quintessentially human, the vehicle for a religious and poetic penetration into the nature of reality such as Dante and Hopkins and Maritain and Callaghan and McLuhan possessed. I was sure that the creative imagination of the artist — poet, painter, composer, architect — was exactly what Wordsworth and Coleridge had called it — "reason in her most exalted mood." About 1952 I was introduced to Morley Callaghan by his son Michael, one of my closest friends and afterwards best man at my wedding to Noreen Mallory, whom I had met in the Callaghans' home. Between 1952 and 1955 Noreen and I used to visit the Callaghans' house on Dale Avenue and listen to Morley talking late into the night. He was working on the early drafts of *The Many-Coloured Cost* . He knew that I hoped to become a writer and he would talk to Noreen and me almost as though we were fellow artists. What we talked about was largely the question of how the great invisible realities, supernatural charity, the action of Divine Grace, sinless innocence might be delivered in fictional narrative. I was convinced that *The Loved and the Lost* was a saint's legend, that its heroine Peggy Sanderson had been touched by the Holy Spirit and was suffering through martyrdom, like Father Dowling in *Such Is My Beloved* and Kip Caley in *More Joy in Heaven* . All three were full of Being, overflowing with supernatural charity; all three were human beings chosen to suffer and be saved in a special charismatic way, as examples of salvation history. I came away from these talks with Morley convinced that the analogy of proportionality united all things within the creative act of Love. "Many waters cannot quench Love."

Simultaneously, Marshall's interest in analogical thought had communicated itself to some of the scholars known in those days as the New Critics, W. K. Wimsatt, Cleanth Brooks, Francis Fergusson and Allen Tate, among the most distinguished members of the new criticism. Allen Tate, poet and critic, who became a Catholic at this time, brought his understanding of Coleridgean poetics with him to the Institute for Advanced Study at Princeton where, about 1952, he had many conversations with Jacques Maritain who was in residence at the institute at the same moment. The chief result of these conversations was Maritain's Mellon Lectures, which appeared in 1953 as the book *Creative Intuition in Art and Poetry*, which finally made me sure that what I'd been thinking about as the union of the active illuminating intellect and the creative imagination was in truth what Maritain and Tate and Wimsatt and Brooks and Fergusson would all have agreed to call "creative intuition." I went ahead with my thesis work and submitted the text in 1955 as "Theories of Imagination in English Thinkers, 1650-1798." The work was accepted by the university in November of that year, and I became a duly licensed teacher of literature, the vocation that has been the support of my life. I thought foolishly that I'd come to the end of my thinking about the active intellect, the creative imagination, creative intuition, and the work of Maritain, Callaghan and McLuhan, which had fused in my mind into a way of seizing the real. I was wrong.

Three weeks after I presented my thesis for the doctorate I sat down at a desk in my office at Saint Joseph College, West Hartford, Connecticut, and typed out the opening pages of a novel called *God Rest You Merry*. It seemed to me that I might deliver my imaginings of reality, the interrelations of all existents brought to birth by the fire of Divine Love, in fictional narration. I knew I was not a systematic thinker of any sort. I was an artist and I hoped that my art would unfold in that holy fire. I owe the sources of that hope to Morley and Marshall. I believe that they shared it. I still live in that hope.

A good way to end.